ABADDON, AND MAHANAIM;

OR,

Dæmons and Guardian Angels.

BY

JOSEPH F. BERG, D. D.,

Pastor of the Second Reformed Protestant Dutch Church of Philadelphia.

PHILADELPHIA:
HIGGINS & PERKINPINE, 40 N. FOURTH ST.
1856.

KING & BAIRD, PRINTERS, SANSOM ST.

PREFACE.

THE subject of demoniacal influence has become almost practically ignored in the prevalent theology of our day. The reaction consequent upon a period of most grotesque superstition has probably produced this result, and the design of the ensuing pages is to restore the teachings of the Scriptures to their proper place in the creed of Christian faith, or at least to contribute to that end, by presenting those acknowledged truths of the Bible which unquestionably bear upon this topic. The present period in the history of the Church and of the world has been signalized by an almost unprecedented attention, amounting to fanaticism, to so-called spiritual manifestations. That these phenomena are in very many instances the merest tricks of mountebanks who have imposed on popular credulity, is no doubt true, but that they are all to be resolved into this explanation, is, to my mind, not so clear. I believe it to be altogether possible, that a real demoniacal influence may, in many instances be put forth, and though I have never witnessed any of the performances of the alleged "spirits," and what is more, never intend to be a party to any such exhibition, I still deem myself prepared to try the spirits whether they be of God, by a plain appeal to the great test of truth, to which all things spiritual must be brought at last. The very language of the apostle in the passage just cited, is peculiarly impressive and significant. Of course, we need not be told what every commentator will tell us, respecting the meaning of the writer, but is it not altogether possible, and even probable, that there was a more literal import in his mind than is usually supposed? Is it not true that Satan rules in the children of disobedience, and that he has legions of evil spirits at his command, all, like himself, engaged in the infernal work of deceiving that they may destroy? Is it not true, that Satan has facilities for reaching the human mind and influencing human passions, and even directing human agency, which are shared by the hosts at his command? Why, then, should it seem an improbable thing, that the apostle should have designed these very words, as a warning against that malign influence, which is so often and so fatally exerted to the betrayal and ruin of souls? To my mind, this idea appears to be the legitimate expression of the sense of the apostle. Besides, if I mistake not, there are direct and specific predictions bearing upon this very thing, as eminently characteristic of the present period. This is "the Time of the End." It is *then*, or rather, *now*, that "Satan comes down in great wrath, knowing that his time is short." With reference to this very period, the time of the sixth and seventh vials, it is written, that "spirits of dæmons" go forth "working wonders," and if I err in applying these predictions to the so-called spiritual manifestation, I have at least, as yet, seen no evidence sufficient to prove that it is an error. I know, we have had philosophical and psychological treatises almost without number, but they are as great a marvel, and their explanations are as unintelligible, as the very subject of which they treat. I greatly prefer the Bible philosophy, though in the estimation of the wise and learned, this may be proof of the want of a philosophical mind. Hegel's naïve and characteristic confession is worthy of commemoration. "I have found," says he, "but one man who understands me, and *he* does not!" Probably, it is owing to the neglect of the authoritative teachings of the Sacred Scriptures, that the impression has come to prevail by a kind of tacit prescription, which consigns all belief in the dæmoniacal influence to the fellowship of the Salem witchcraft and kindred delusions, and assumes as a thing to be taken for granted, that no diabolical or dæmoniacal influences can be exerted, under the New Testament dispensation, even if they ever had existence under the Old, which some seem almost to doubt. Should this be so, we must commend to such persons, a closer study of the Scriptures, as an infallible corrective of this error. No truth is more clearly part of the revealed counsel of God than this to which we have already adverted. No doctrine stands out in bolder relief upon the sacred page, and is reiterated with more frequent and solemn warnings, than that which teaches the direct, constant and malignant activity of the hosts of hell, in deceiving, betraying, tormenting and destroying the souls of men.

In close relation with the exposition of the Scriptural doctrine of dæmoniacal influence is the opposite and comforting truth, that Holy Angels are sent forth as ministering spirits to them who are heirs of salvation. This is a truth which all Christians hold, and though in some respects a distinct dogma, its relation to the system of Christian doctrine renders its consideration apposite in connection with the subject of the malign influences which Satan and his angels continually exert. Jacob called the place where the angels of God met him,

Mahanaim, *i. e.*, "two camps," indicating two companies of angels, one as the vanguard, the other as the rearguard of the pilgrim of faith.

The object proposed in the following pages is to condense the teachings of the word of God upon these subjects, and then to leave the matter with the mind and conscience and heart of those who may be interested in this inquiry.

Philadelphia, December 6, 1855.

EPHESIANS IV. 27.

27. Neither give place to the devil.

2 KINGS VI. 15, 16, 17.

15. And when the servant of the man of God was risen early, and gone forth, behold, an host compassed the city both with horses and chariots. And his servant said unto him, Alas, my master! how shall we do?

16. And he answered, Fear not: for they that *be* with us *are* more than they that *be* with them.

17. And Elisha prayed and said, LORD, I pray thee, open his eyes, that he may see. And the LORD opened the eyes of the young man; and he saw: and, behold, the mountain *was* full of horses and chariots of fire round about Elisha.

JOB I. 6, 7.

6. Now there was a day when the sons of God came to present themselves before the LORD, and Satan came also among them.

7. And the LORD said unto Satan, Whence comest thou? Then Satan answered the LORD and said, From going to and fro in the earth, and from walking up and down in it.

CHAPTER I.

SATAN, THE ENEMY.

THIS admonition of the apostle Paul has special reference to the government of the passions. It stands in connection with a number of practical suggestions respecting the life and conversation of believers, and constitutes one of those terse, summary and comprehensive precepts, in which the writings of the inspired apostle abound. "By no means give place to the devil." The Christian is required to stand on his guard, to watch against the encroachments of the adversary, and never to yield to his solicitations, or to his assaults. As the soldier of Jesus Christ, set for the defence and maintenance of the station entrusted to him, he is to hold it at any personal sacrifice, and by no means to give place to the devil. This is evidently the import of the text.

The Scriptures plainly teach the existence of a mighty apostate angel, who bends all the resources of his power to the grand purpose of deceiving, betraying and destroying the souls of men. Hence the frequency and earnestness with which holy men of God, who spake as they were moved by the Holy Ghost, warn the Church and the world against his wiles, are to be regarded, not as the offspring of exaggerated apprehension, but as words of truth and soberness. In intellect, in strength, in powers of perception, in subtlety, in all the faculties which make a created spirit formidable, he towers far above the hosts of darkness, who obey and follow him as their leader and prince. The titles ascribed to him in the Sacred Scriptures all illustrate his malignity and his power. They imply that he is destitute of every good principle—that he falters not in view of any expedient which may help him to consummate his schemes of ruin. He is to be deterred by no suggestions of pity; a stranger alike to truth and love, he lies in wait to deceive, and by all the devices of infernal cunning, he toils, tasking his mighty energies to the utmost, in order to delude, degrade and devour the victims of his perfidious cruelty. In the Old Testament writings, he is called BELIAL, a Hebrew word, which signifies literally "good for nothing," one who is reprobate to all good. He is called SATAN, the *adversary*, denoting his implacable enmity to God and man; LUCIFER, the *morning star*, indicating the brilliancy of his intellect; LEVIATHAN, the *crocodile*, from his insatiate cruelty. In the New Testament he is spoken of as the DEVIL, or the Calumniator, because he is the accuser of the brethren; as the Tempter, as a Liar and a Murderer from the beginning; as the Old Serpent, who deceived Eve by his subtlety, and as "the Deceiver." He is represented in the apocalyptic vision as the Great Dragon—as the Angel of the Bottomless Pit, whose name is, in Hebrew, Abaddon, and in Greek Apollyon, the DESTROYER. The apostle Paul styles him "the Prince of the power of the air," alluding probably to the limits within which Satan is confined with his angels and subjects; and the same apostle designates him as the *God of this world*, because wicked men serve him, are blinded by him, and led captive at his will. These are the principal titles ascribed to the devil in the Scriptures, and sufficiently indicate his character and power. Before proceeding to inquire into the modes by which the influence of Satan is exerted, and its ancient and modern manifestations, it will be proper to make a few preliminary remarks. Strictly speaking, the term Devil is a proper noun, or the name applicable only to the leader of the fallen angels. Our version speaks of devils as though there were many, but the original word is *daimonia*, dæmons, which properly means the spirits of departed human beings, and is employed in the Scriptures of the New Testament to designate, indifferently, fallen angels, and disembodied spirits who are made the objects of idolatrous worship. The word Διαβολος, devil, in the New Testament is never used in the original to designate any other being but SATAN, except in a single instance, and then it is employed by Christ, figuratively, to denote the enormity of the crime of Judas, who betrayed him. "Have not I chosen you twelve, and one of you is *a devil.*" In every instance in which the term "devils" occurs as a plural noun in the New Testament, it will be seen that the original word is dæmons. This distinction will be found of practical importance in the course of this discussion.

Again, when we speak of Satan, we must guard against the error of supposing that he is ubiquitous. He is not Omnipresent; if he were, he would be God. He is not even every where present on the earth, at the same time. He possesses the power of going to and fro over the earth, and doubtless can change his place of sojourn with the rapidity of thought. This is implied by the words of Christ—"I saw Satan, fall like lightning from heaven." In the book of Job, (i. 6, 7,) we read, "Now there was a day when the sons of God came to present themselves before the Lord, and Satan came with them. And the Lord said to Satan, whence comest *thou?* Then Satan answered the

Lord and said, 'From going to and fro in the earth and from walking up and down in it.'" To the same purport is the saying of the apostle, "Be sober, be vigilant, for your adversary, the devil, *goeth about* as a roaring lion, seeking whom he may devour." A spirit, not being confined within the material barriers which impede the motions of an embodied creature, may pass with inconceivable rapidity from one place to another, but the presence of a spiritual being is limited by its finite nature. God is the Spirit whose presence fills the universe. This is an exclusive attribute of the Deity. He shares this glory with no creature, and therefore we are not to conceive in any way that this faculty of ubiquity pertains to Satan.

The Prince of Darkness is not alone in his condemnation, for we read of Satan and his angels, and the Scriptures lead us to infer that the number of the hosts who own him as their sovereign, is beyond computation great. Inferior to him in capacity, of different grades in authority, intellect, and strength, they are all devilish in the malice and hatred with which they unite in tempting and deceiving, and in seeking to subvert and destroy the foundations of human happiness and peace. In the epistle to the Ephesians, St. Paul teaches this doctrine explicitly. He represents the Church of the living God, and each believer for himself, as engaged in a constant warfare with the powers of darkness. For "we wrestle not with flesh and blood"—if we did, the danger would be less—but we "wrestle *not* with flesh and blood, but against principalities, against powers, against the rulers of the darkness of this world—against wicked spirits in high places." The Devil is therefore a usurper. He has occupied this earth with his armies, and claims to be its god. Here he has set up the standard of rebellion against the King of kings and the Lord of lords. The banners of the Prince of Peace float from all the battlements and towers of Zion, displaying, upon their pure white field, the ensigns of light and love--and Satan builds his strong-holds in the dark places of the earth, and from all the habitations of cruelty, flings in defiance of King Jesus, his flag upon the breeze, and musters the powers of darkness and the principalities of hell to fight against the Lord and his annointed.

We are not to imagine, however, that the spirit-world is peopled solely by malignant beings or fallen angels. God forbid! Jehovah is the God of Sebaoth—the Lord of Hosts. There are angels who excel in strength, cherubim radiant with knowledge; seraphim burning with love, principalities and powers, ministers of his who do his will, flying at the command of Jehovah Jesus—guarding his Church—protecting his saints—ministering to them who are the heirs of salvation. These crowd around the Lord Jesus Christ and hail him as their Prince. These constitute his shining retinue—attend him in his conquests, and celebrate his triumphs and his praise. Left to ourselves, we could not make a stand against the armies of hell, but Christ is with us. The angel of the Lord encampeth round about them that fear him, and delivereth them. When the King of Syria warred against Israel, finding himself thwarted by the prophet Elisha, he sent horses and chariots, and a great host, and by night encompassed the city of Dotham, where the man of God dwelt. "And when the servant of the prophet was risen early, and gone forth, behold a host encompassed the city, both with horses and chariots. And his servant said unto him, 'Alas! my master, how shall we do?' And he answered, 'Fear not: for they that are with us are more than they that are with them. And Elisha prayed, and said, 'Lord, I pray thee open his eyes that he may see.' And the Lord opened the eyes of the young man and he saw, and behold the mountain was full of horses, and chariots of fire round about Elisha." 2 Kings vi. 18.

The ministry of angels, whether of light or darkness, is a most important doctrine of the Scriptures; and it is remarkable, considering the prominence given to it in the word of God, that it should occupy so small a space in the theological writings and the popular teachings of the present day. It is a theme which is comparatively rarely introduced into the pulpit and it would seem as though much which is distinctly revealed in the oracles of God, for the instruction and warning of believers, had been, by a kind of tacit consent, practically ignored, as though it were obsolete truth, having reference wholly to a by-gone age. The cause of this neglect is probably to be found in the persuasion that the doctrine of Satanic influences has, in former times, been grossly perverted, and so distorted and exaggerated, as to minister to superstition and fanaticism, rather than to real edification. This is certainly an extreme which must be avoided. It is itself a development of Satan's cunning; but after running the truth beyond the conservative limits of Scripture into wild extravagance and folly, he has changed the mode of assault, and now under the plea of superior light and knowledge, he seeks to discard important doctrines, that he may practise, not upon the fears, but the presumption of men, and prosper to their ruin, without rebuke. We believe we are prepared to show, that many of the so-called developments of spiritual science, which have been vaunted as modern discoveries, destined to exert a powerful influence as new light from the spirit world, even, and as a new revelation from heaven, are nothing more and nothing less, than emanations of old darkness, devilish devices, known to the heathen, thousands of years ago, practised by them and by apostate Jews, under the old dispensation, forbidden by the law of Moses under pain of death, and denounced in the New Testament, almost in the last chapter of the Bible, with the fearful menace of eternal damnation. It is written, "The fearful, and unbelieving, and the abominable, and whore-mongers, and SORCERERS, and idolators, and all liars, shall have their part in the lake which burneth with fire and brimstone; which is the second death." (Rev. xxi. 8.) Shall we through infidel sneers at fanaticism, stultify the solemn declarations of the book of God? Shall we yield to the ignorance or prejudices of persons, who never make the testimony of the Lord the man of their counsel? What would this be, but giving place to the devil? There is a most intimate connection between the prosperity of the church, the growth in grace of believers, and the proper and seasonable administration of the truth. God has ordained his truth as the spiritual nourishment of the soul, and in the temptations peculiar to every age, he has declared that his word is a lamp to the Christian pilgrim's feet. Hence David thankfully avows, "By the word of thy lips I have kept me from the paths of the destroyer."

Is it not therefore the duty of every minister of the Lord Jesus, who would be true to his master, to his trust, and to his conscience, like the prophet Habakkuk, to get him up into his tower and watch, and when the Providence of God points out a growing evil, to warn the faithful against THE ENEMY?

To some minds, the very announcement of the subject which we would discuss, indicates a want of sound philosophy. With them, Satan is the object of ridicule. They regard the Devil as occupying a position in the system of revelation similar to the clown in a pantomime. With them, Satan is the staple of the coarse jest and the ribald profanity, which betrays a heart hardened by the deceitfulness of sin. Let them see to it, that the words of Christ witness not against them: "Wo unto you that laugh now, for ye shall mourn and weep." That Satan does exert a most powerful influence for evil upon the minds of men, is a truth which God himself has revealed, and which cannot therefore be ignored without damage to Christian faith. Let me say, moreover, that my object is simply to expound what *the Scriptures* teach on the subject of Satanic influences. I have no new theory to broach on any matters connected with them, neither am I a believer in all the marvellous stories, with which the foolish and credulous are wont to frighten those who are like-minded with themselves; but I believe the Bible is a revelation from God, therefore no portion of the truth which it contains can be neglected or overlooked, without practical loss to the Church. The plan which we propose is to review, seriatim, the various phases of Satanic influence described in the Scriptures, and to compare them with the modern manifestations of his power.

The popular idea seems to be that since Christ Jesus was manifested, that he might destroy the works of the devil, Satan has been shorn of his strength, and that he is not permitted in this age to exercise the arts by which he formerly prevailed. To a certain extent, this is true, but there is reason to fear that he has regained some of the ground which he had lost, and it is certain that he still exercises tremendous power. In examining the records of the Bible on this subject, we obtain certain general principles, which it will be well to define and secure firmly in our minds for future reference.

1. *Satan possesses the faculty or the power of deluding the minds and even the senses of men.* We may

safely set down the proposition, that Satan never has wrought and never can work a *miracle.* This power belongs to God alone. He employs miracles as special vouchers to the genuineness and authenticity of his revelations, and we may rest assured, that He never will permit Satan to work miracles in support of a lie. This would be to invalidate the divine testimony and to confound and silence the inspired witnesses of God's own appointment. A miracle implies a suspension of the ordinary laws of nature. It is a work effected, in a manner foreign to the established method of providence, by God himself, in attestation of the authority of messengers of his own appointment. Whilst we affirm, however, that Satan never has been permitted to work miracles, we must remember that he has powers vastly superior to any that pertain to merely human agency, and that things which are utterly beyond the reach of human strength, are yet within the compass of the devil's ability. Power may be superhuman, and still not miraculous. If Satan cannot work real miracles, he can counterfeit them so adroitly, that the deception cannot easily be detected. A single illustration of this proposition may suffice. When Moses was sent to the Court of Pharaoh, with the authoritative demand, LET MY PEOPLE GO, the Lord instructed him that in answer to Pharaoh's request, "show a miracle," he should direct Aaron to cast his rod at the king's feet, and it should become a serpent. The servants of Jehovah fulfilled their commission, and the rod which Aaron cast at Pharaoh's feet became a serpent. The Egyptian sorcerers and magicians were called in, "and they also did in like manner with their *enchantments*, for they cast down every man his rod, and they became serpents, but Aaron's rod swallowed up their rods." Though this was designed as proof that the power of the God of Israel transcended that of the magicians, yet Pharaoh was not convinced. And now the Lord begins to vex Egypt with terrible plagues. The waters in every stream, and river, and pond, and pool, throughout the land, are turned into blood—but still the delusion of the devil continues—for we read, "the magicians of Egypt did so with their *enchantments*." Again Jehovah commands his servant, "Go unto Pharaoh and say unto him, Let my people go, that they may serve me." Again Pharaoh refuses. The rod of Aaron is stretched over the streams, and rivers, and ponds, and frogs come up and cover the land of Egypt—but still we read "the magicians did so with their enchantments, and brought up frogs upon the land of Egypt."

It is evident from the context, that Pharaoh

taunted the servants of Jehovah with the skill of his magicians, for when the plague became intolerable, and he called for Moses and Aaron, and said "Entreat the Lord for me"—*take away the plague and I will let the people go.* Moses replies, "*Glory over me*—when shall I entreat for thee and thy servants and thy people to destroy the frogs from thee and thy houses, that they may remain in the river only? And he said, To-morrow. And he said, Be it according to thy word; that thou mayest know that there is none like unto the Lord our God." The plague was removed; but Pharaoh was not yet subdued. Another plague came upon the land. Aaron, in obedience to divine direction, stretched out his rod and smote the dust of the earth, and it became lice in man and in beast, throughout all the land of Egypt. "And the magicians did so with their enchantments to bring forth lice, but they could not. Then the magicians said unto Pharaoh, *This* is the finger of God." (Exod. viii.). Here is a confession that the arts by which they had produced the semblance of the former miracles, were NOT of God, and we must conclude, either that they were tricks and juggling impostures, or that they were delusive appearances, wrought by the interposition of the devil, or that they were realities produced by the operation of natural laws, which the devil may make subservient to his own purposes. If Satan was permitted to exercise this power in the case of Pharoah, the superior might of Jehovah shone forth the more resplendently from the contrast. Besides, when men deliberately reject the truth, and prefer unrighteousness and falsehood to it, the apostle declares, for this very cause God permits them to fall into strong delusion, that they may believe a lie and perish in the belief of it. The very delusion in which they trust, becomes a judgment upon their unbelief and impenitence. For my own part, I prefer the opinion, that the wonders wrought by the magicians before Pharaoh were delusions—optical delusions—produced by the agency of Satan. It is not more strange that he should have power to deceive the eyes, than that he should be able to blind the minds of them that believe not. The evidence of miracles is a divine condescension to the philosophical necessities of our nature. The conviction that miracles are the true attestation of the presence of divine power, is constitutional with human reason. Hence the foundation of every religion, whether true or false, is found to rest in a belief of miracles. It is a principle which constitutes the root of every form of faith or belief which the human mind has ever received. Thus, even enthusiasts and impostors have always claimed to work miracles. In the days of Elymas, down through the age of Mahomet, to the Mormon leader Joseph Smith, all false prophets have claimed miraculous powers. This claim is the fruit of a felt necessity in the human mind. Call it an intuition, or an induction of reason, God is its author. It exists wherever man is found, and is interwoven with the very texture of human nature. Hence the demand for miracles as an attestation of the divine origin of the Revelation which God has given, is a philosophical necessity. The power of Satan is beyond doubt superhuman. He may, therefore, work many things which to men may appear miraculous, because they are superhuman, but they are not supernatural, for Satan as a creature is under law. He may understand, and doubtless does understand, the principles of the operations of law better than we possibly can in our present state; but his agency is circumscribed by the limits of laws, which he cannot overstep, though their subordinate results may be under his control. He is the "Prince of the power of the air."

In the case of the miracles wrought in Egypt, there was a manifest contest between the priests of Satan and the servants of God; and it was essential therefore to show the superiority of the power of the God of Israel over the gods of Egypt. The series of miracles increased consecutively in severity, and by the fourth miracle, lice came upon every man and beast in Egypt. "Now, if it be remembered," says Glieg, "that no one could approach the altars of Egypt, upon whom so impure an insect harbored: and that the priests, to guard against the slightest risk of contamination, wore only linen garments, and shaved their heads and bodies every day, or every third day, according to Herodotus, the severity of this miracle, as a judgment upon Egyptian idolatry, may be imagined. Whilst it lasted no act of worship could be performed, and so keenly was this felt, that the very magicians exclaimed, 'this is the finger of God.'"

2. *Another preliminary proposition which we would establish is this, that Satanic influence is not necessarily confined to the sphere of spirit, but extends also to material objects.* In proof of this, we might adduce the demoniacal possessions cited in Scriptures, but these we waive for the present, as they constitute a distinct subject of inquiry. We are our selves, in our very persons, living witnesses of the power which spirit exercises over organized matter. Does not the spirit that is in this body exert constant influence upon it? The hand does not move

itself; it is the animating spirit which controls it. It is not the eye that *sees*—the eye is merely the organ which conveys the image of material objects to the mind. The tongue and all the apparatus of articulation, are only the instruments by which the soul gives utterance to thought. When a man dies, though all these organs are in perfect development, the eye is sightless, the hand has forgotten its cunning, the tongue is dumb. The spirit has departed, and the body is dead. Abstractly, there is nothing absurd, therefore, in the idea, that a spirit can control matter. God is a Spirit, and he is the Creator and Preserver of the universe. Satan also may exercise his power upon material objects; always, however, within the limits which God has assigned. The devil was permitted to lay his hand upon all that Job possessed. He stirred up the Sabeans, and they fell upon his servants and slew them, and drove away his oxen. He caused fire to fall from heaven and burn up the sheep and the shepherds. He incited the Chaldeans, and they fell upon the camels and carried them away, and slew the servants with the edge of the sword. He brought from the wilderness a great wind and smote the four corners of the house in which Job's sons were feasting, and it fell upon the young men, and in an instant they were dead. And when tidings of all these calamities had been brought to Job, he arose and rent his mantle, and shaved his head, and fell down and worshipped, and said, "The Lord gave and the Lord hath taken away, blessed be the name of the Lord." Again Satan appears when the sons of God came to present themselves before the Lord —and again Jehovah asks "Whence comest thou?" and the same answer is returned, "From going to and fro in the earth and from walking up and down in it." For the trial of the faith and patience of Job, God permits the enemy to touch his bone and his flesh, "and the Lord said unto Satan, Behold he is in thine hand, but spare his life." So went Satan forth from the presence of the Lord, and smote Job with sore boils from the sole of his feet to his crown."

Not without reason does our Saviour teach his disciples daily to pray, "Deliver us from the evil one."

Follower of Jesus, be sober, be vigilant, "Satan desires to have you that he may sift you as wheat.

Ye, who despise the great salvation, awake! The devil goeth about as a roaring lion, seeking whom he may devour, and can *you* sleep? Behold the long-suffering of God. Were it not that his hand restrains the fiends of hell, who follow you as ravening wolves pursue their prey, this very hour, they would rend your soul from the body and drag you down to chains and darkness with them to wait the judgment of the great day.

REVELATION XII. 7–9.

7. And there was war in heaven: Michael and his angels fought against the dragon: and the dragon fought and his angels.

8. And prevailed not; neither was their place found any more in heaven.

9. And the great dragon was cast out, that old serpent, called the Devil, and Satan, which deceiveth the whole world: he was cast out into the earth, and his angels were cast out with him.

CHAPTER II.

SATAN, A TEMPTER.

WAR in heaven! This is a startling annunciation. We are wont to regard heaven as the habitation of quietness and peace. Such it is; such it ever will be. The cry of them that strive for the mastery—the tumult of combatants struggling for their homes and their altars shall never be heard in heaven; but there *has been* discord even among the first-born of God's creatures. Satan, the Devil, lifted the standard of rebellion in a world which till then was the Paradise of God, and Sin entered the hallowed precincts of Jehovah's empire. Temptation, pride, the lust of place and power overthrew a host of angels. They fell with Satan their Prince from their allegiance, "and there was war in heaven. Michael and his angels fought against the dragon, and the dragon fought and his angels." Is this language merely symbolical, or is it the narrative of an actual crisis in the history of heaven? We think it is both. Without a doubt it is literally and symbolically true. It may be that this passage which describes the war in heaven is a symbol of the conflict of the gospel with the Pagan powers which it overthrew. This we will not dispute, but the symbol is indicative also of a literal truth. A constant conflict is waged between the powers of light and darkness. Good and evil angels surround us. We have friends in the spirit world who minister as God's messengers to the heirs of salvation. Angels who excel in strength are sent forth on errands of love to them who hope in his mercy. And we have foes in the spirit world also, mighty and malignant, filled with the rancor and spite of hell, seducing spirits, whose infernal office-work is the ruin of the children of disobedience. This "war in heaven" is but another name for the constant and conflicting influences exerted by these spiritual antagonists upon the human mind. Power, strength, dominion, are attributes of spirit. When Satan and his legions became apostates, in view of the throne of heaven, and in the very precincts of Jehovah's courts, they contended for the thrones and principalities and places which they had held in the period of their obedience. With the impudence of hell, they fought for the possession of heaven, and the hosts of God resisted them. "Michael and his angels fought." We ask, who is this Michael—the Prince who leads the holy angels in the encounter with the Dragon and his legions? Some affirm, this Prince is the Lord Jesus Christ. This opinion is open to objections, which are not devoid of weight.

The name occurs three times in the Old Testament, in the book of Daniel, and twice in the New Testament Scripture, and it is contended, *all* that is stated respecting this personage must agree with the titles, the attributes and the position of Jesus Christ, or the theory which identifies Michael and the Saviour, must be rejected. The name occurs, for the first time, in the vision of Daniel (chap. x.), in which he sees "a certain man clothed in linen, whose loins were girded with fine gold of Uphaz—his body was like the beryl, and his face as the appearance of lightning, and his eyes as lamps of fire, and his arms and his feet like in color to polished brass, and the voice of his words like the voice of a multitude." The vision of this celestial visitor overwhelmed the prophet, and "there remained no strength in *him*." The angel touches him, as prostrate and powerless Daniel lies with his face to the ground—speaks lovingly to him—"O Daniel, a man greatly beloved, understand the words that I speak unto thee, and stand upright; for unto thee I am now sent. And I stood trembling. —Then he said unto me, Fear not, Daniel; for from the first day that thou didst set thine heart to understand, and to chasten thyself before thy God, thy words were heard, and I am come for thy words.—But the prince of the Kingdom of Persia withstood me one and twenty days: but lo, MICHAEL, *one of the chief princes*, came to help me; and I remained there with the kings of Persia." The heavenly messenger proceeds to tell what shall befall the people (the Jews) in the latter days, and after stating that he must return to fight with the prince of Persia, he says, "I will show thee that which is noted in the Scripture of truth, and there is none that holdeth with me in these things but MICHAEL, *your prince*." Again, the name occurs in Daniel xii. 1. "At that time shall MICHAEL stand up, *the great prince*, which standeth for the children of thy people: and there shall be a time of trouble, such as never was since there was a nation," &c.

In the New Testament we find the name Michael in the epistle of St. Jude. MICHAEL, the *Archangel*, when contending with the devil, he disputed about the body of Moses, durst not bring against him a railing accusation, but said, *the Lord rebuke thee*." The body of the Moses, here spoken of, is not the dead body—or the bones of the man of God, but the Jewish law or institutions, the body of Jewish divinity — and the idea is that Michael and Satan disputed about points in Hebrew law.

Papists put some stress upon this passage, and lay it down as a foundation for their ridiculous relic worship—a most unfortunate quotation, truly, for we may infer that the devil wished to get the body of Moses to make holy relics of it, but Michael withstood him. This, however, is merely in passing. The last mention made of Michael occurs in our text, in which he appears as an angelic leader. It will be admitted, that much which is here predicated of Michael, may with truth apply to Jesus Christ. The very meaning of the name Michael, "*Who is like the Lord?*" seems to indicate this identity. The fact that there is but *one* archangel spoken of in Scripture may also be adduced as evidence to the same purport, and yet there are difficulties in the way of this theory. The language in Dan. x. it is argued, can hardly consist with the idea that MICHAEL is Christ. "MICHAEL, *one of the chief princes came to help me.*" Here he is described as ONE of the chief, but Christ is THE CHIEF Prince, with whom no other can compare. 2. Though there is but one archangel spoken of in the Bible, there is an evident distinction affirmed by the apostle, (1 Thess. iv. 16), "For the Lord himself shall descend from heaven with a shout, with the voice of the archangel, and with the trump of God." Jesus Christ himself shall shout, and they that are in the grave shall hear the summons—the archangel shall echo that voice, and angels flying over the whole earth shall re-echo it, severing the wicked from among the just, and gathering God's elect together. 3. St. Jude says, MICHAEL *durst* not bring a railing accusation (τολμᾶν) against Satan, but said "THE LORD rebuke thee." But why this appeal to *the Lord*, if Michael were himself Jehovah?

The strongest passage in support of the theory that Michael, the prince, is our Lord, is *that* in Dan. xii. in which it is said, "Michael shall stand up, the great prince which standest for the children of thy people"—but it is agreed again, there is nothing here inconsistent with the idea, that Michael, the Archangel, was commissioned to work great deliverances for, or to avert great dangers from the Lord's people. Some prefer, therefore, that interpretation which harmonizes all the declarations of the Scripture, respecting this personage, and accordingly regard Michael as the Prince of holy Angels—the created antagonist of Satan—equal to the Angel of the bottomless pit, in all the endowments which can give power to a created spirit, and crowned with holiness the most resplendent glory of all. And is there not a beautiful analogy in the thought that holy angels have a mighty prince of their own nature, who vies even with Lucifer—the apostate morning star, and quick and brilliant as the lightning, to which the Saviour compares Satan, meets the Great Adversary and baffles him in his assaults upon the children of God's Israel? If Lucifer became a wandering star, and was sent down to wound the blackness of darkness for ever, Michael, the Archangel, held fast his allegiance to the throne of God, and excellent in strength, waits as the Messenger of Jehovah Jesus, the King of angels and of men, to do his holy will and for ever to rejoice in obedience, as his highest honor.

Notwithstanding the difficulties which seem to invest this question, we deem the weight of evidence as decidedly in favor of the view which represents our Saviour as the Prince of angels, from the fact, that the prophecy in Daniel, which represents Michael the great prince standing for the children of God's Israel, synchronises and corresponds with the prophecy in the Apocalypse of St. John, in which the Lamb stands upon Mount Sion. And may not this whole subject possibly suggest the reason why holy angels regard the Redeemer of men, with a personal reverence more tender and endearing than that which springs solely from holy veneration of their Creator? If Michael and Jesus be one, then the Saviour of men led on the hosts of heaven in their warfare against the prince of darkness, when Satan was cast down with all the angels that sinned.

"There was war in heaven! Michael and his angels fought against the dragon; and the dragon fought and his angels, and prevailed not, neither was there place found any more in heaven. And the great dragon was cast out into the earth, and his angels were cast out with him."*

Thus do the oracles of God account for the appearance upon this earth of the Arch-Deceiver, who was a liar and a murderer from the beginning. The creation of man constituted a new era in the world's history. Driven from heaven, shunned and abhorred by all holy beings, Satan appeared in Paradise, and as the Old Serpent, who deceiveth the world, commenced his career in Eden, as the TEMPTER.

I. First, then, in his character as the Tempter, we would regard the Great Enemy of God and man. *Observe his subtlety.*—He comes not in his proper form. He appears not as an Angel of darkness, bearing the scars of divine wrath. He comes not in his true character as the Adversary of all good. This would have sent a thrill of horror though the heart of his victims. He approaches the scenes of innocence, cautiously—stealthily as the serpent glides on its errand of death. Not as the Prince of hell, attended with a gloomy array of malignant angels, does he come to make war upon human innocence

* There is often a dualism in the symbols of prophecy.

and demand submission to his power, but as a playful, guileless, harmless creature, he nestles by the side of Eve. Satan gave to the viper its deadly venom; when God created the serpent, like all the glorious Maker's works, it was good. Why, then, shall Eve fear it? Why shall she fear any thing? Hist! The wily serpent speaks. "Has God indeed said ye shall not eat of every tree of the garden?" A denial of the truth, is, most artfully implied; the lie is insinuated, but so that it works its mischief, without exciting alarm. If repulsed, the Tempter may admit, that it is truth, and deny the intent to challenge it. Eve apprehended no danger, and yet her peril was imminent. The very suggestion of a doubt, when she herself had heard Jehovah's mandate, should have made her start with horror and amazement. She is parleying with Satan, and he has already gained an advantage, for he has obtained a hearing. She answers, "We may eat of the fruit of the trees of the garden, but of the fruit of the tree which is in the midst of the garden, God hath said, Ye shall not eat of it, neither shall ye touch it, lest ye die." See again, the Tempter's subtlety. He chooses a time when Eve is alone. Two are better than one, and he may hope the more securely to corrupt and ruin the representatives of our race, if he assails them singly. Perhaps, if Adam were there, a suspicion of some foul design might cross the mind of one or the other, and like birds frightened by an awkward fowler, his prey might escape. Emboldened by toleration, he advances. She is not alarmed by th unwonted circumstance, that the serpent whispers to her out of the dust, and suggests a doubt respecting the existence of a well-known precept. He questions, she responds.

2. *Observe, the Tempter's effrontery.* — "And the Serpent said unto the woman, Ye shall not surely die!" He assumes the attitude of an open antagonist of God, still with the semblance of friendship and affection for her. Does not denial of God's truth startle her, and blanch her cheek with horror? Alas! She has sinned already. Her fall is already secured. When she can hear the charge of falsehood uttered against Jehovah, without quivering with anguish in every nerve, her allegiance must already be shaken. The Tempter knows it. With malignant haste, he follows up his advantage. She has heard him impeach Jehovah's truth—and she still listens to him. Then, she will not be terrified if the adversary assails the goodness of the kind Father, who has invested Eden with all its beauties and made happiness and love beam out of every flower that blooms at her feet, and shines forth from all the ten thousand glories that sparkles on the bosom of

a sinless world. Yes—if she can bear that impeachment of a Father's truthfulness, she will endure any imputation that the devil may cast upon her God. Now he stands forth revealed, as the slanderer, the liar-murderer. "Ye shall not surely die. For God doth know, that in the day ye eat thereof, then your eyes shall be opened; and ye shall be as gods, knowing good and evil." Did not Satan's voice falter when this blasphemy was uttered? The unblushing liar masks his hatred of God under the flimsy veil of affectionate sympathy for the inmates of Eden. *They are suffering great wrong—and the law of God is in the way of their progress—and he presents himself as the Reformer, who can teach them to be as gods, able to judge for themselves, and to discern between good and evil.* The Tempter's flattery is successful. Eve looks wistfully towards the forbidden tree. The fruit that loads its boughs is pleasant to the eyes—the branches bend invitingly to her hands, and her doubts and hesitation yield to the persuasion of the Serpent. "And when the woman saw that the tree was good for food, and that it was pleasant to the eyes, and a tree to be desired to make one wise, she took of the fruit thereof, and did eat; and gave also unto her husband with her, and he did eat." Thus sin entered into the world, and death by sin. Shame and fear appear as the first fruits of transgression.

With conscious guilt, they hide from the presence of the Lord. Eden is no longer the abode of innocence; it is polluted by the presence of sinners, and God drives them from it, guards its entrance, and sends them forth to look upon a world, which has lost the glorious impress of holiness, and is cursed for the wickedness of them that dwell in it. The first temptation is the type of the devil's wiles. It is the great model, after which the devices, wherewith he prevails over human credulity, self-love, and pride are fashioned. Look at the arts by which Satan now tempts men from their obedience to the law of God. Do they not all bear the devil's mark, and prove that they are copies of the pattern framed in Eden? We wonder, that men can be so foolish as to imagine that God will stultify his own character, by promulgating a law that has no sanctions—but we need not wonder. The Devil seduced Adam and Eve from original righteousness by this very device. He is the first, and he is the great Universalist preacher! He first suggests a doubt, whether it comports with the goodness of God to affix the penalty of death as the wages of transgression. *Has God indeed said so?* And when place is given to this suggestion, he goes a step farther and denies the existence of the penalty. "Ye shall not surely die." What! is God less wise than man? What believer in the silly quibbles of Universalism will accept a bond that expresses no obligation and no forfeiture? What human law-giver or legislature ever framed a law without attaching a penalty?

Let a man be persuaded that this folly pertains to God's legislation and though the statutes of the Lord are as plainly before his eyes, as the precept prohibiting all access to the forbidden tree was in the memory of the tenants of Eden, he will, like them, be prepared, as the next step, to deny the truth of divine revelation altogether, and to listen to the blasphemer, who with the impudent malice and falsehood of the Arch-deceiver and Seducer, avows as his creed, "God doth know, that in the day ye eat thereof, your eyes shall be opened and ye shall be as gods, knowing good and evil." Now is not this the very counterpart of the position assumed by the infidel reformers of our day? Is not their cry substantially this? *The Bible is the great stumbling block in the way of modern improvement! It stands right in the very path of human progress. Then away with it! It is the engine of priestcraft! For what can be plainer that if you take away the Bible, you undermine the Church, and crush the ministry beneath its ruins?*

Thus, we have a renewal of the old device of the devil, in the question proposed by the merciful philanthropists, who say to the murderer, "Hath God indeed said, thou shalt surely be put to death?" We have a renewal of Satan's falsehood in the denial that God's law affixes any such penalty to the crime of murder, and there are thousands who are ready with open mouth to echo the words of Satan, "Ye shall not surely die!" and with the effrontery of the devil himself to declare, "The Bible teaches that the murderer shall be permitted to live, because Christ came to destroy the old law, though Christ himself proclaims, I came not to destroy the law, but to fulfil it! Till heaven and earth pass, not one jot or tittle of the law shall fail—all shall be fulfilled! What more natural than the invariable result of this falsifying of the record? They who embark upon this gulf-stream float out into the open sea of infidelity, and make utter shipwreck of the faith. You see them, after walking in the counsel of the ungodly, and standing in the way of sinners, taking their seat, at last, in due time, among the scornful, and blaspheming the name and the law of God, without remorse or shame! Beware of any scheme of *human progress* which discards the way of holiness marked out in the book of God—believe none of its honied pro mises of social improvement and intellectual advancement—trust not the lying Tempter when he whispers "ye shall be as gods, knowing good and evil"—lest sinning as Satan sinned through pride in the court of heaven, sinning as Adam sinned, as Eve sinned in Eden, ye fall into the condemnation of the devil.

We have not space to review the history of Satan's career as the Tempter, as we find it recorded in the book of God. We know how he has triumphed over thousands of the great and noble of the world—how, by his subtlety, he has peopled the dark domains of hell, and lured, betrayed and ruined countless generations of men. Many wise and many mighty have been slain by him! Oh! this earth is slippery with the blood, and white with the bleaching bones of his victims. Against which of God's saints has he not at some time prevailed to cast them down, though never to destroy them? Noah fell under the power of temptation, whilst the earth was yet reeking with the exhalations of the flood—Lot sinned while the smoke of Sodom and Gomorrah was rising from the plain, like the smoke of a furnace—Abraham, the Father of the Faithful, dissembled before Abimelech—Moses, with all his meekness, was petulant at the waters of Meribah—David, the man after God's own heart, yielded to the devil and sinned in the matter of Uriah, the Hittite. Who, that lives, or strives to live a Christian life, does not realize daily the necessity of praying as our Lord taught his disciples to pray, "Lead us not into temptation but deliver us from the evil one?" That wicked one addresses temptations to the tastes of the most refined, as readily as to the sensual appetites of the most depraved. Eve saw that the fruit of the tree was pleasant to the eyes, and she took of the fruit and did eat. The pleasures of sin are garnished with the most attractive hues—like the bloom upon the fruit of death which hung in Eden on the forbidden tree. Oh! guard the avenues of sense, lest they prove gates by which Satan may enter the soul. "Look not thou upon the wine when it is red, when it moveth itself aright, when it giveth his color in the cup; at the last it biteth like a serpent, and stingeth like an adder." Avoid the door around which they loiter, who tarry long at the wine. Stay not to admire the glare that shines invitingly through the stained glass, for there Satan holds his revel, and his guests are sinking into the depths of hell. Yea, "Watch and pray, lest ye enter into temptation!" Shrink from the first approach of sin. Listen not to the plea of the devil, that it is but a little one. Abstain from all appearance of evil.

We may not dismiss the view of Satan's character as the Tempter, without remembering, that as such he assailed our Saviour. Jesus was led up of the Spirit into the wilderness, to be tempted of the devil (Matt. iv.). The adversary chooses his time, when our Lord, weary and exhausted with fasting, was an hungered. Then, he comes, taunting Christ with an expression of doubt respecting his Messiahship, and claiming a miracle, which would argue distrust in divine providence, as the proof that Jesus was the Son of God. "If thou *be* the Son of God, command that these stones be made bread!" Was it not evidently the design of the devil to ruffle the placid temper of our Saviour, to take advantage of the infirmities of our nature, and through the weakness of the body to wound the spirit of our Lord? How insulting is the base insinuation, "Command these stones to be made bread, or I will not believe that thou art the Son of God!" How impudent the demand, as though Christ must be at special pains to convince the deceiver! But the Saviour meets him with a rebuke which foils the enemy. "It is written, man shall not live by bread alone, but by every word that proceedeth out of the mouth of God." Man lives not alone by bread, but by obeying the commands of God. Language could not convey a more pungent reproof to the Arch-Rebel against

God. Satan quailed under it. "Then the devil taketh him up into the holy city, and setteth him on a pinnacle of the temple, and saith unto him, if thou be the Son of God, cast thyself down, for it is written, He shall give his angels charge concerning thee: and in their hands they shall bear thee up, lest at any time thou dash thy foot against a stone." If Jesus will not yield to distrust, peradventure he may be cajoled into presumption. If HE quoted Scripture, the devil will quote it also, but Satan quotes it falsely. He omits the important words, "in all thy ways," which qualify the promise and guard it against presumptuous abuse. He shall give his angels charge *to keep thee* "IN ALL THY WAYS." The believer does not rush blindly into danger, and then expect deliverance on the ground of covenant promises. This is not his way. Therefore Christ beats him back again with the answer, "It is written again, Thou shalt not tempt the Lord thy God." "Again, the devil taketh him up into an exceeding high mountain, and showeth him all the kingdoms of the world, and the glory of them: and saith, all these things will I give thee, if thou wilt fall down and worship me." Ambition—the lust of power—cast Satan down from heaven, but see how wickedness, how apostasy from God, debases every moral faculty. Satan offers to Christ that which already pertained to the Redeemer as the Creator of the ends of the earth! The usurper offers what he has no right to give away—the usurper offers to the rightful Sovereign the dominion which pertains to him, as the Maker of heaven and earth—and on what terms? We shudder at the blasphemous proposal — on condition that Jesus Christ shall acknowledge the devil's supremacy—become an idolater — fall down and worship the Fiend of the bottomless pit! Never did the malice of hell devise a more blasphemous insult. It was the outpouring of Satanic hatred, roused to madness by the purity of Jesus. With quiet dignity the Saviour maintains his power, and issues the command, which Satan must obey, "Get thee behind me, Satan—for it is written, thou shalt worship the Lord thy God and him only shalt thou serve! Then the devil leaveth him, and behold angels came and ministered unto him."

Remember, it is written, and Christ's example and experience prove the truth of the divine promise; yea, in every hour of temptation, remember, it is written—

"Resist the devil and he will flee from you."—(James iv. 7.)

LUKE IV. 33–35.

And in the synagogue there was a man, which had a spirit of an unclean devil, and cried out with a loud voice, saying, Let us alone; what have we to do with thee, thou Jesus of Nazareth? art thou come to destroy us? I know thee who thou art; the Holy One of God. And Jesus rebuked him, saying, Hold thy peace, and come out of him. And when the devil had thrown him in the midst, he came out of him, and hurt him not.

CHAPTER III.

SATAN, A TYRANT.

No sooner had Satan gained his first victory in Eden, than he addressed himself to the work of consummating the ruin in which he designed to involve the whole human family. He doubtless knew the position in which Adam stood as the representative of the race; that upon that issue of the probation in Paradise, depended results of the most momentous consequences to countless generations of Adam's posterity. "Who can bring a clean thing out of an unclean? Not one." Every tree produces fruit of its own kind. "Do men gather figs of thistles, or grapes of thorns?" However diverse the philosophical speculations of men may be—however keenly they may desire to discriminate—and however jealous of theological terms, all who read the Scriptures with unbiassed mind, acknowledge, that Adam by the fall, became not only himself a sinner, but the head of a sinful race. Human nature was corrupted by the first transgression, so that even they who are regenerate must acknowledge with the holy apostle: "By nature we are the children of wrath, even as others." The Bible teaches, and universal experience proves, that it is the nature of sin to increase unto more ungodliness. "When lust hath conceived, it bringeth forth sin, and sin, when it is finished, bringeth forth death." So it was in the beginning. The first man was a transgressor, and the first who was born of woman was a murderer. How terrible is the development of sin. How rapidly does it advance and grow, until it works itself out in death. After the first advantage gained by the enemy, his subsequent success was comparatively easy. Before the expulsion from Eden, Adam, with his guilty partner, trembling in his hiding place, was compelled to honor the voice which sent a thrill of dismay to his inmost soul, as its tones echoed through the walks of Eden, "Adam, where art thou?" He comes forth—alas! how changed! No longer the noble, confiding, guileless man, meeting his Maker as a son, who reveres his Father, but with the stealthy, downcast look of an ungrateful, faithless servant. It was the cool of the day—evening had set in; the hour in which they were wont to meet the Lord God in the garden. They heard his voice, "and Adam and his wife hid themselves from the presence of the Lord God, amongst the trees of the garden." Oh! the efforts of sinners to shun the presence of the all-seeing God are vain. Could they escape to heaven, still God is there and he sees them—could they hide in the darkest recesses of the earth, still the eye of God beams upon them. If they seek a refuge in hell—even there, the hand of the Lord shall find them out. "And the Lord God called unto Adam, and said, Where art thou? And he said, I heard thy voice in the garden, and I was afraid, because I was naked; and I hid myself. And the Lord said, Hast thou eaten of the tree whereof I commanded thee that thou shouldest not eat? And the man said, The woman whom thou gavest to be with me, she gave me of the tree and I did eat. And the Lord God said unto the woman, What is this that thou hast done? And the woman said, The serpent beguiled me and I did eat." See how subterfuge and prevarication followed in the wake of sin; "God made man upright, but he hath sought out many inventions,"—sordid, selfish inventions! It was true, that Adam was ashamed and hid himself—but it was not the whole truth. He prevaricated when he substituted a single effect for the real cause. Paradoxical as it may seem, men may say words which in themselves are true, and yet they may lie, by aiming to conceal the truth. And when the *whole truth* is extorted, as it will be from every sinner, when he stands in judgment before God, see how selfishness absorbs the best affections of the heart, and seeks to palliate its own sin by impleading another. "The *woman* whom *thou* gavest to be with me, she gave me of the tree and I did eat." A generous nature would have scorned to lay the burden of its own wrong upon another. But enough, sin makes man selfish, and therefore the great precept of that Messiah, whose advent was promised in Eden, whilst Adam and his wife still lingered within its enclosure—the great command upon which Jesus makes discipleship depend, is "DENY THYSELF!" When love to God and love to man reign over the heart, in obedience to the two great commandments, then the soul is regenerated and redeemed from the bondage of the devil.

After Satan had obtained that first hold in Eden upon the obedience of mankind, the work of subjugation made rapid progress. His grand design was to bring man, the last of God's intelligent creation, wholly under his yoke. Thus the tempter throws off the mask of friendship—and having first deceived Eve by the specious promise of moral and intellectual progress, and ultimate advancement to a God-like nature, he proves himself the tyrant who seeks to lord it over the souls and bodies of men—this transition from the tempter to the tyrant is easy and natural. As the tyrant, who torments those whom he first seduces, we shall view Satan in the present chapter.

The text presents us with one of the most fearful forms in which the power of the devil has ever been exhibited on earth. Instances of demoniacal influence and possession are repeatedly adduced in the writings of the evangelists, and the narratives are couched in such language, that it is impossible for any honest mind to escape the conviction, or to evade the plain and necessary inference, that the evangelists intended to describe real facts. They are not dealing in metaphor, but they are describing events, which they assure us actually took place. A grosser absurdity can hardly be committed, than to assert that the distinct narratives, illustrating the power which Jesus Christ exercised over evil spirits, are all to be understood as figurative expressions—or myths—fabulous stories—designed to show his power in expelling depraved passions from the mind, or in healing diseases of the body. And yet this is the position which some have ventured to assume, and which they are in fact obliged to take, in order to escape certain inferences, fatal to their whole scheme of false doctrine. Infidels generally have a very marked aversion to those portions of the sacred Scriptures which treat of the personality and agency of the devil and his angels; and the reason of all this is obvious. If the existence of Satan can be proved from the Bible, and if the authority of the Bible, as a divine revelation be admitted, then it becomes absolutely impossible for any sane man to shut his eyes against the truth, that there is also a HELL, which is the appropriate—the final and everlasting habitation of Satan and his angels. Hence you find, that those who deny the one always are compelled eventually to deny the other also. Truly, they have a weary time of it! To keep up a hypocritical appearance of reverence for the Scriptures, and at the same time erase from the oracles of God its plainest doctrines, and *reverently* to change the most momentous truths into myths or fables, requires some ingenuity and no little effrontery! And methinks they who can lend their faculties to such miserable drudgery, would do well to inquire, whether they may not themselves be affording deplorable evidence of the reality and power of Satanic influence by the zeal with which they labour to disprove its existence.

Let us apply the ordinary tests of criticism to any of the narratives of demoniacal possession recorded in the New Testament, and the conclusion will be irresistible, that they were real and not imaginary evils. In the gospel, we find distinct narratives relating to demoniacal possessions. That the subjects of those fearful influences were not simply lunatics is evident.

1. The evangelist Matthew distinguishes between those that were possessed with devils, (dæmons,) and those that were lunatic. "And his fame went out throughout all Syria: and they brought unto him all sick people that were taken with divers diseases and torments, and those which were possessed with devils, and those which were lunatic, and those that had the palsy, and he healed them." Matt. iv. 24.

Those who were possessed, differed from persons oppressed by forms of insanity in the accuracy with which they reasoned. Amid all the diversities of mania to which a commission of lunacy is awarded, we find two great principles established in the phenomena of insanity. The unhappy subjects of mental disease, in the ordinary affairs of life, either reason correctly on false premises, or they reason incorrectly on right grounds, or they blend right and wrong in inextricable confusion. The dæmoniacs, on the contrary, reasoned correctly—they assumed right premises and deduced right inferences. Their words were always adapted to the occasion, without any sort of incoherency. They were consistent in their knowledge and in their language. They had clear views of the character and person of Christ. The dæmons declared, "We know thee, who thou art, the Holy One of God." Though the malignant influence of the dæmons was exhibited in the torture to which they subjected the victims of their power, both in mind and body, disturbing and destroying the faculties and senses of the possessed, they were nevertheless intelligent and accountable agents.

3. Again, Jesus Christ addresses them as intelligent beings, and as such they reply to him. This plainly involves the idea of personality. How unutterably ridiculous do the narratives of the evangelists appear, if we adopt the idea that demoniacal possessions involve nothing preternatural. Indeed, where any circumstances are added, they are invariably of a description to show that the case was extraordinary in its nature. Are we told that these possessions were mere forms of bodily disease? Then we have the absurdity staring us in the face, that diseases cry out, and argue and protest. Take a passage, (Luke iv. 41,) "And devils, (dæmons) also came out of many, crying out and saying, Thou art Christ, the Son of God! And he, rebuking them, suffered them not to speak; for they knew that he was Christ." Now, if the word *dæmon* means *diseases*, we may substitute the one for the other, and the passage will read: "And diseases also came

out of many, crying out and saying, &c. And he, rebuking the diseases, suffered not the diseases to speak, for the diseases knew that he was Christ." You may apply this test to every case of malignant spiritual possession recorded in the Scriptures, and substitute any thing or every thing that the ingenuity of man can invent in place of the proper text of the sacred writings, and you involve the entire narrative in absurdity. We are therefore shut up to the acknowledgment, that the possessions spoken of in the New Testament, are really what the language purports to make them. Indeed, among the portions of the word of God, which are clear, beyond the possibility of any misunderstanding, save that which is wilful, those which relate to the personality, power, and direct agency of Satan and his angels upon the minds of men, are among the most manifest. Some will tell you that the scene, in which the Tempter appears in Eden, is all a myth —a kind of allegory, meaning just anything at all you please to make of it. If that is an allegory, how is it that the apostle Paul quotes the fact of the serpent's beguiling Eve as real? His words come home to these allegorists with great pungency: "I fear lest by any means as the serpent beguiled Eve through his subtilty, so *your* minds should be corrupted from the simplicity that is in Christ."

We are told the devils believe and tremble. Can this be affirmed of any other than rational, intelligent agency? May we not justly and clearly discern a device of Satan, in the attempt to make little of his power, and even to deny his existence altogether? For, what can be more plain, than the results of this phase of unbelief? They who are unwilling to admit the fact of Satan's existence, or the reality of his agency, or the malign influences of the principalities and powers of darkness, will give themselves no concern about these spiritual foes, and will the more readily fall a prey to the subtilty of the Wicked One.

The fact therefore, we hold to be established, that the demoniacal possessions described in the Sacred Scriptures, were real occupancies of the persons of individuals by malignant spirits, who held the bodies and souls, the senses and faculties of the victims of satanic power, completely under control; tormenting them, making life a burden, and rendering their subjects a horror to themselves and to all around them. At the period of the advent of Christ, Satan's empire upon the earth was probably more firmly established than at any former time since the flood. By gradual advances, he had acquired tremendous ascendancy over the minds of men, and through this avenue, their bodies also were transformed into strongholds, which were garrisoned at some times even by a legion of dæmons. Thus on one occasion, we find these evil spirits declaring, "Our name is Legion, for we are many."

Mary Magdalene is mentioned as one "out of whom went seven dæmons." It is a fact, equally worthy of note, that at no period previous to the advent of Christ, had the Sadducean form of infidelity so strong a hold upon the Jewish mind. The Sadducees denied the proper existence of spirits altogether—they believed neither in angel nor devil—and they had a multitude of proselytes to their unbelief. The Pharisees and Sadducees divided the control over the popular faith or creed of the Jewish nation. The former, like the Papists of our day, made void the law of God by their traditions, and the latter set the truth of God at defiance by their blank infidelity, and yet both coalesce, as infidelity and popery do now, in opposition to the pure doctrine of Christ. It was, when Satan had set himself up as the god of this world, when he felt most secure in his possession, that Christ Jesus appeared in human form. He was manifested that he might destroy the works of the devil—wrest the sceptre from the grasp of the usurper, and drag him back to the chains from which he had escaped. Accordingly, among the very first acts of Christ's public ministry, the casting out of dæmons is recorded by the Evangelists, and the fearful extent to which this spiritual malady prevailed at this crisis, is manifest from the frequency not only of single narratives of cases of possession, but also from the repeated declaration that multitudes of persons thus afflicted were brought to Jesus to be healed. Thus we read: (Matt. viii. 16,) " When the evening was come, they brought unto him *many* that were possessed with devils; (dæmons) and he cast out the spirits with his word." Again, St. Luke says, " Dæmons also came out of *many*, crying out and saying, " Thou art Christ the Son of God." (Luke iv. 41.) Christ Jesus gave his disciples authority over all devils, to cast them out, and when the seventy returned who had been sent forth to preach the kingdom of God, and to work miracles, in proof of the authenticity of their commission, they came rejoicing to Christ, and saying, " Lord, even the dæmons are subject to us."

How pitiable was the condition of the wretched victims of Satanic power! The faculties of mind and body, became so many engines of torture, by which the malignant fiends tormented the possessed. Imagine the feelings of a mother, whose once lovely daughter has fallen under the power of Satan. Moved by an impulse unseen but irresistible, she falls foaming upon the ground, convulsed in every limb—shrieking with distorted features, and utterly unable to control her language or her actions! With what earnestness did that poor Syro-Phœnician woman appeal to Christ, casting herself at the Saviour's feet, and crying out in the anguish of a mother's love for a suffering daughter—"Lord, help me!" See how she clings to the Saviour's feet, when for the trial of her faith, he delays the answer to her prayer! How she utters amid sobs and tears her broken lamentation—"My daughter is grievously vexed with a dæmon!" And when Christ tells her that his mission is to the lost sheep of the House of Israel, and that she cannot therefore claim any help from him by her own right—she, trembling with anxiety, lest after all, her suit may be denied, and yet trusting to the mercy of Jesus, humbly answers, "Truth, Lord, yet the dogs eat of the crumbs that fall from the master's table!" Then, when faith like gold refined comes forth bright from the ordeal, the Saviour bids her be of good cheer. "Oh! woman, great is thy faith—be it unto thee even as thou wilt, and her daughter was made whole from that hour." How joyous the meeting, when returning to her home, she finds her daughter rescued from the power of the devil! What imagination can conceive the aggregate of wretchedness—the untold misery resulting from the direct agency of the devil, in these fearful exhibitions of despotic power! Think of the husband—the father of a household, severed from his wife and children, fleeing from the habitations of the living, seeking death, whilst death flees from him, and taking up his dwelling amid the tombs. Then rushing forth, despite of all the resistance of his own will, to maltreat, to wound and to maim any who come within his reach—cutting himself, in the paroxysm of Satanic phrensy, until, covered with wounds, and faint with the loss of blood, he sinks foaming and exhausted to the earth! How precious is the office-work of Christ, in this aspect, as the destroyer of the devil's power! What gladness did his mission of mercy diffuse throughout the families of Israel, whom he delivered from the yoke of this intolerable bondage. Oh! If Christ Jesus had not pitied this revolted world—had he left it to the dominion of the king of the bottomless pit—it would long ere this have been set on fire of hell, and Satan and his angels would have been incarnate in the human family! Some, who would be counted wise men, or scribes well instructed in the gospel, will scout the idea of Satan's ability to reach the minds of men, so as to hold communication with them—as though it were in itself a thing impossible, or so improbable as to savor of superstition, for a moment to admit it. But the Scriptures teach that more than this has actually occurred—that Satan cannot only find means of reaching the minds of men, but that he also has been able to control by his agency their bodies, and literally to possess himself of their faculties, and in a word, of their persons in its complex nature. The greater surely involves the less, and the Scriptures plainly teach that both the one and the other are not only possible, but are actually matters of historical fact. Of this, however, we shall say more when we speak of Satan in his character as an idol or false god.

They who would argue on the ground of mere reason against the possibility of this nefarious influence, must ignore the plainest principles established by experience and observation. We are wont to regard the spirit-world, as at an immense distance from us; but even if the Scriptures were silent upon the topic, we have no just warrant for any such conclusion. We know that there are good and bad embodied spirits on the earth, in other words, there are good and bad men and women. And what is a man? He is a deathless spirit, united for a little season to a body of dying matter. What are we in our persons but incarnate spirits? and why is it unphilosophical to suppose that spirits out of the body good and bad, may surround us? Why is it in itself irrational to suppose that we are actors in scenes to which angels and dæmons are spectators? This conclusion, to which even reason may arrive, revelation and experience establish upon an immoveable basis. The Apostle declares, we are a spectacle to men and to angels, and he represents the Christian as running for the prize of celestial glory, encompassed by a great cloud of witnesses. Observation confirms this declaration, and proves that we are encircled with spiritual beings, who are all interested in our progress and destiny. In confirmation of this, let the phenomena be adduced so frequently exhibited in the dying hours, both of the believer, calmly awaiting the summons to his Father's house, and of the wicked man, who is surprised by the sudden inroad of mortal sickness, and in his wickedness is driven away. Adopting the belief not authorized by the Scriptures, that this body, the present dwelling-place of the spirit, shuts out our spiritual vision from objects which are not material, and hangs like a curtain between the world of sense and the spirit-world, we are prepared to account for facts, which otherwise are not so easily explained.

I remember well, when a child, separated by the wide ocean from my parents, among my schoolmates was a little boy, whose father was engaged with mine in preaching the gospel to the poor negroes in the West Indies. My heart yearned over him; he was so modest and guileless; so amiable and full of artless affection, and withal so small and delicate, and we were both so far from home that there was to me an unsual attraction about him; and I never shall forget how he pined away like a blighted flower, and was taken to "the sick-room." The sickness was unto death—and as he lay, propped with pillows on his bed, his pale and wasted face—his panting breath—his eyes sparkling with that unearthly light, that gleams through the windows of the soul, like rays from a brighter world, all told plainly that he was going home. There was a sudden flush upon his features. He raised his little hand and whispered, "Oh, listen! That sweet music!" Then starting up, his face shining with rapture, he followed with his hands the objects which were before his vision, repeating, "See! see those holy Angels! Let me go—dress me, let me go with them!" And he did go with them. Is it not of such, that Jesus says, "Their angels do always behold the face of my Father who is in heaven?" Among the sweetest thoughts of death, which ever filled my heart, from childhood until now, are those which come whispering from the grave of my little friend. How soft and quiet that earthy bed, with its coverlet of green turf, in which the weary body sleeps, whilst the freed spirit goes away to dwell with Jesus and the holy angels! The sweet strains of the little hymn which we sang at his grave, sound as though they were still trembling on the air of that summer evening:

"Happy soul! thy days are ended,
All thy mourning days below,
Thou, by angel-guards attended,
Didst to Jesus' presence go."

Now, why is it, that these phenomena are so common in the death-bed experience of them who love the Lord Jesus Christ? Say you these are the fruits of a distempered mind? But is it not strange, that amid all this *wild wandering* of the spirit, there is perfect consistency with the revealings of God's holy word? And how is it, that the wicked man in his death, has no sound of heavenly melody charming his ears, and no sight of holy angels, hovering around his pillow? Why is it, that instead of these, images of terror float before his glaring eyes and fill the soul with horror and dismay? Is it not, because when men are dying, the curtain of this body is gradually lifted up, and the soul hitherto not cognizant of the presence of attending spirits, looks out into the eternal world, and stamps an impress of its realities upon the fading senses? And when the spirit is poised upon the confines of the two worlds, and its heaven or its hell is already begun, why need we wonder that the righteous has hope and glory in his death, whilst the wicked are trembling in overwhelming terror and despair? Let this suggest a closing thought.

In the midst of wrath, the Lord remembers mercy, and doubtless God has permitted Satan and his angels to torment the souls and bodies of men upon this earth, that he might rebuke the unbelief and presumption of them who deny the very existence of Satan's person and power, and who, like the Sadducees, reject the most momentous truths. He has poured a flood of evidence so overwhelming, that it sweeps away the cavils of the self-willed rejecters of his truth, that they may take warning and escape the everlasting torment and tyranny of hell. If, even here, Satan could make life a burden, and pervert every faculty of mind and body, into a fountain of pain and sorrow; how, then, can any soul endure the terrors of that tremendous sentence, "Depart, ye cursed, into everlasting fire, prepared for the devil and his angels?"

2 CORINTHIANS IV. 4.

In whom the god of this world hath blinded the minds of them which believe not, lest the light of the glorious gospel of Christ, who is the image of God, should shine unto them.

CHAPTER IV.

SATAN, A FALSE GOD.

HUMAN depravity is manifested in no development of sin more fearfully, than in the supreme obedience which is paid by the wicked to the suggestions of the evil one. The Scriptures declare, that he "rules in the children of disobedience," that they "are led captive by the devil, at his will." These are expressions of tremendous import. They declare, as powerfully as language can do it, the strong hold which the great enemy possesses upon the affections and passions of men. They imply a complete prostration of the liberty in which his subjects so often make their boast. The will is enslaved. The understanding is deluded. The conscience is perverted. The affections are in bondage. To my mind, there is no exhibition of the doctrine of human depravity more terrible than this. Probably no passages of Scripture can be adduced, which assert it with greater emphasis than those which describe the moral influence and agency of Satan upon the minds of men. The enemies of God imagine that they are their own masters. Strange delusion! They cast off allegiance to Him, whose right it is to reign; they declare their independence of his government and law, and whilst they vauntingly exclaim, "our lips are our own; who is lord over us?" they are in fact proclaiming their allegiance to Satan. This is a truth which is not usually appreciated as it should be. They who have never sued for the pardon proffered in the Gospel, and who are consequently not at peace with God, are scarcely conscious of the terrible reality that they are serving, not so much themselves, as they are obeying the commands of Satan. Does not this thought invest the grosser forms of vice with peculiar virulence and atrocity? The blasphemer who hesitates not to profane the name of the Most High, and who in sheer recklessness—in the very wantonness of indifference to sacred things—avows his contempt for all that is holy, proclaims with the very breath that fills his mouth with oaths and curses, his complete subjection to the power of the devil. The blasphemies which flow from the lips of the wicked man in his wrath, are so many acts of worship offered to "the god of this world." This character of Satan is the culminating point of his usurpation. He can make no higher pretension than this. He offers himself as the god of the wicked. And wh are the wicked? Moral men are ready to reply: the drunkard, who debases his intellect, stupifies or maddens his brain with strong drink, who heeds not the claims of his heart-broken wife and famishing children, who goes from the place of carousal reeling in loathsome intoxication to the comfortless home, in which his trembling family seek a shelter in vain from the ebullitions of capricious fury—the drunkard, they reply, is a wicked man. They say truly, for such he is. They tell us again: the licentious man, who triumphs over the virtue of his victim and boasts of his success—and the vile pander, who spreads a net for the feet of innocence, and insidiously corrupts the morals and the tastes of her own sex—these are wicked. Truly! they are abominations! They reply again: the corrupters of public morals, who make the mind familiar with printed impurity, and outrage all decency in their shameless infamy, are wicked. We admit it. They will point to the man who extorts the last penny from the worn hand of honest poverty, to the mean tradesman, who screws as with a vice, the reward of the poor woman's daily toil down to the veriest pittance, for which he can exact days of unremitting industry, and they will load him with epithets of reproach. He deserves them. They will paint the character of the deliberate slanderer, who maliciously distorts the truth, who makes a lie and loves it, and who revels with delight amid the ruins of the reputation which he has destroyed, and then turn from the picture with loathing and disgust, and we acknowledge, their indignation is righteous. But, we ask, are these and such as these, the only subjects of Satan? I would not undervalue morality. I know it is better that men should be temperate, and chaste, and honest, and prudent in speech and conduct, than that they should betray their parentage and show that they are of their father the devil, by practising vices which are the opposites of temperance and purity, of justice and truth—but a man may possess all these virtues and more, and still be under the dominion of the devil. The Scriptures present a higher standard. They demand no less than a complete surrender of the heart to God, in order to emancipation from the power of the evil one. You are either "of this world," or you are "of the household of God;" either a fellow-citizen with the saints, or an alien from the commonwealth of Israel There is no middle ground. You are either a child of God, or you belong to the children of disobedience, in whom Satan rules. "If you walk not by faith in Jesus," you are blinded by Satan. For "the god of this world hath blinded the minds of them that believe not." A favorite device of the devil in all ages, has been, to counterfeit the institutions and the ordinances of God, and to endeavour to impair, and if possible, neutralize the moral influence of Christian virtues by base and contemptible caricatures.

Jehovah established ORACLES, at which he heard the vows and prayers of his people, and gave answers through his prophets to the inquiries of their judges and kings. The word *oracle* is used in the Old Testament Scriptures to denote the mercy-seat. The original Hebrew word *caphoreth*, derived from *caphar* as its root, properly means a *covering*, and its significance will be apparent at once, in its application to the cover of the ark of the covenant, the sacred chest, in which the laws of the covenant were enclosed. "And thou shalt make two cherubims of gold, of beaten work shalt thou make them, in the two ends of the mercy-seat. And make one cherub on the one end, and the other cherub on the other end: even of the mercy-seat shall ye make the cherubims on the two ends thereof. And the cherubims shall stretch forth their wings on high, covering the mercy-seat with their wings, and their faces shall look one to another; toward the mercy-seat shall the faces of the cherubims be."—(Exod. xxv. 18–20.) It also denotes the SANCTUARY, the

Holy of Holies, in which the ark was deposited. "And against the wall of the house he built chambers round about, against the walls of the house round about, both of the temple and of the oracle; and he made chambers round about." "And he built twenty cubits on the sides of the house, both the floor and the walls with boards of cedar: he even built them for it within, even for the oracle, even for the most holy place. And the house, that is, the temple before it, was forty cubits long."—(1 Kings vi. 5, 16, 17.)

The Jews had several distinct means of ascertaining the will of God, in any special crisis or emergency, apart from the ordinary teachings of the revealed law. Such were the direct communications which were made by the Almighty to Moses, and delivered orally by the great prophet of the law to the children of Israel. "With him will I speak mouth to mouth, even apparently, and not in dark speeches, and the similitude of the Lord shall he behold."—(Num. xii. 8.)

Prophetical dreams were also employed, in order to indicate to the servants and prophets of the Lord, particular events which were to happen either to themselves or to the Jewish nation. A well known instance of this occurs in the history of Joseph, to whom God revealed his future promotion over his brethren, and afterwards again, when a prisoner in Pharaoh's dungeon, Joseph was apprised of the will of God by similar instrumentality. (See Gen. xxxvii. 5, 6, and Gen. xl.)

Prophetical visions were also employed. These differed from dreams, and are frequently mentioned as distinct from them, not only in the writings of the prophets, but also in the historical portions of the Scriptures, both in the Old and New Testament. Thus Joel declares: "It shall come to pass afterward, that I will pour out my Spirit upon all flesh; and your sons and your daughters shall prophesy, your *old* men shall dream dreams, and your *young* men shall see visions." Thus the LORD encouraged Abraham in a vision. (Gen. xv. 1.) And again in the visions of the night, he appeared to the patriarch Jacob, "and spake unto Israel, and said, Jacob! Jacob! and he said, Here am I. And he said, I am God, the God of thy father, fear not to go down into Egypt; for I will there make of thee a great nation." (Gen. xlvi. 2, 3, &c. Consult also, Numb. xii. 5, 6.)

The Urim and Thummim which was in the ephod, or pectoral or breast-plate of the high priest, is also called an oracle or oracles, because it endowed with supernatural knowledge the high priest who wore it. From Joshua's time to the building of the temple at Jerusalem, the consulting of the Urim and Thummim was a common mode of inquiring of the Lord. Two remarkable instances are recorded in the history of David. "And David knew that Saul secretly practised mischief against him: and he said to Abiathar, the priest, Bring hither the ephod. Then said David, O Lord God of Israel, thy servant hath certainly heard that Saul seeketh to come to Keilah, to destroy the city for my sake. Will the men of Keilah deliver me up into his hand? Will Saul come down, as thy servant hath heard? O Lord God of Israel, I beseech thee, tell thy servant. And the Lord said, He will come down. Then said David, Will the men of Keilah deliver me and my men into the hand of Saul? And the Lord said, They will deliver thee up."--(1 Saml. xxiii. 9–12.) Again, at the spoiling of Ziklag by the Amalekites, when David was greatly distressed, he "said to Abiathar the priest, Abimelech's son, I pray thee, bring me hither the ephod, and Abiathar brought the ephod to David. And David inquired of the Lord, saying, Shall I pursue after this troop? Shall I overtake them? And he answered him, Pursue, for thou shalt surely overtake them, and without fail, recover all."—(1 Saml. xxx. 7, 8.)

After the completion of the temple, the usual

mode of ascertaining the divine will was by consulting the ordained prophets of Jehovah. There was then, no unnecessary connection either with certain specified times, or particular places, or even with the personal character of the priest who uttered these predictions. The High priest when clothed with the ephod gave a true answer, whatever might be the manner of his life. He spoke as he was directed, and no doubt at times gave an answer, the full import of which he did not himself understand. A remarkable instance in point is furnished in the incidents attending the arraignment of Christ before the tribunal of Caiaphas, the Jewish High-priest. He pronounced an oracle relating to the Saviour, which he did not himself understand in its real import. "Ye know nothing at all, nor consider that it is expedient for us, that one man should die for the people, and that the whole nation perish not. And this *he spake not of himself*, but being High-priest that year, he prophesied that Jesus should die for the people." That was the last utterance of the Urim and Thummim. From that hour the voice of prophecy was hushed in Israel. It was meet that it should be so, and that the expiring glory of the ancient oracles of God should bear testimony to the necessity of the sacrifice of Jesus on Calvary, toward which all types and shadows of the Jewish ritual had tended since the giving of the law. Caiaphas hated Jesus, and desired his death, but he bore upon his breast the Urim and Thummim, and ere the light of the ephod is quenched forever, it kindles with dying energy and proclaims the grand truth of the gospel, "It is expedient for us, that one man should die for the people, and that the whole nation perish not."

Now, that the work of Christ is accomplished, save his intercession at the right hand of God's majesty—and the full vindication of his royal prerogative in the subjugation of his enemies—since Jesus Christ has appeared, as the great prophet and high-priest of his Church, and the Holy Spirit has moved upon the hearts of holy men of God, who spake as they were moved by the Holy Ghost, and the will of God is plainly revealed in the Sacred Scriptures, the word—the living, incorruptible word of God has superseded the ancient oracles, and the Spirit of God leads his inquiring and believing people into all truth. "If any of you lack wisdom, let him ask of God, who giveth to all liberally and upbraideth not, and it shall be given him." We inquire of the oracles of God, when we read the Scriptures for our spiritual profit and instruction; when in secret we bow the knee in humble, fervent, faithful supplication; when, in a word, we thankfully use the means of God's appointment, to promote our growth in grace and our increase in the knowledge of our Lord Jesus Christ. God has given to us all the revelation which we need, until the day of the full manifestation of the sons of God in glory, and therefore the canon of sacred writ closes with these solemn words: "I testify to every man that heareth the words of the prophecy of this book; if any man shall add unto these things, God shall add unto him the plagues that are written in this book: and if any man shall take away from the words of the book of this prophecy, God shall take away his part out of the book of life, and out of the holy city, and from the things which are written in this book. He which testifieth these things saith, Surely, I come quickly: Amen! so, come, Lord Jesus."

As Jehovah established his oracles, so Satan set up oracles also. He had them among the heathen nations, who surrounded the Jews, and when by his infernal temptations he seduced the Hebrews from their allegiance, they forsook the oracles of God and went to consult the shrine of Baalzebub. This was insulting Jehovah to his face. Surely, it is blasphemy most horrid, to prefer the altars and the temple of Satan to the ordinances of the living

God! Therefore the anger of God was kindled against his chosen people, when they turned away from the truth to seek after a lie. "And Azariah fell down through a lattice in his upper chamber in Samaria, and was sick: and he sent messengers and said unto them, Go, inquire of Baalzebub, the god of Ekron, whether I shall recover of this disease. But the angel of the Lord said to Elijah the Tishbite, Arise, go up to meet the messengers of the king of Samaria, and say unto them, Is it not because there is not a God in Israel, that ye go to inquire of Baalzebub, the god of Ekron? Now, therefore, thus saith the Lord, thou shalt not come down from that bed, on which thou art gone up, but shalt surely die. And Elijah departed." (2 Kings i. 2–4.) This entire history is the more important from the terrible confirmation which God gave to the truth of his own prophet, when summoned in derision by the captain of fifty, who was sent to apprehend him, "Thou man of God, the king hath said, come down." Elijah sends back the terrible response: "If I be a man of God, then let fire come down from heaven and consume thee and thy fifty. And there came down fire from heaven and consumed him and his fifty." A second captain was sent with another company of fifty, and with still greater effrontery repeats the king's message: "O man of God, thus hath the king said, Come down quickly!" Again Elijah sends back the fearful challenge; "If I be a man of God, let fire come down from heaven and consume thee and thy fifty." And the fire of God came down from heaven and consumed him and his fifty. A third messenger was despatched with another company, but he fell on his knees, acknowledged the power of God, and prayed that their lives might be spared. Elijah, encouraged by the angel of the Lord, went down to the captain, accompanied him to the king, and declared to Ahaziah the message of God, that because he had sent to inquire of Baalzebub, therefore he should not come off his bed, but should surely die. "So he died according to the word of the Lord, which Elijah had spoken." The object of this terrible severity, by which the two companies with their officers were slain, in addition to the death of the king, was manifestly to exhibit the displeasure of Jehovah against the indignity which had been put upon his own oracles, by sending to inquire of the god of Ekron. The heathen oracles of antiquity have, by some, been regarded as having been wholly under the influence of dæmons. In a general sense, they, no doubt, were, but it is altogether probable, that there were several distinct kinds of oracles; some of them were controlled by the illusions of the devil, but others may have been the effects of the juggling and contrivance of the Gentile priests, without any direct Satanic agency in the responses which were uttered.

A remarkable passage illustrative of this truth, is found in 1 Kings, 22. Micaiah, the son of Imlah, a prophet of the Lord, was sent for at the suggestion of Jehoshaphat, who had made an alliance with Ahab. The false prophets whom Ahab consulted, advised that they should go up against Ramoth-Gilead and take it from the Syrians, promising complete success to the expedition. Ahab yielded a reluctant consent to Jehoshaphat's advice, alleging as the reason, that the man prophesied only evil concerning him. Micaiah obeyed the king's summons. "And he said, Hear thou, therefore, the word of the Lord: I saw the Lord sitting on his throne, and all the hosts of heaven standing by him, on his right hand and on his left. And the Lord said, who shall persuade Ahab that he may go up and fall at Ramoth-Gilead? And one said in this manner, and another said in that manner. And there came forth a spirit, and stood before the Lord, and said, I will persuade him. And the Lord said unto him, wherewith? And he said I will be a lying spirit in the mouth of all his prophets. And he said, Thou shalt persuade him and prevail also: go forth and do so." I regard this as a passage of great importance, inasmuch as it seems to settle the fact of the agency of false spirits or lying spirits upon the minds of the prophets, who waited upon the shrines of idol-gods, and I presume this to have been the great principle that was implied, or taught by the figurative vision which Micaiah beheld. This is in accordance also with other didactic portions of Scripture which represent delusion as a judicial punishment for perverse and obstinate adherence to error. "For this cause," says St. Paul, "God shall send them strong delusion, that they shall believe a lie, that they all might be damned who believed not the truth, and had pleasure in unrighteousness." (2 Thes. ii. 11, 12.) Satan was permitted to deceive those, who through hatred of the truth, rejected the counsel of the Lord. "My people would not hearken to me, and Israel would none of me, so I gave them up to their own heart's lust, and they walked in their own counsels." This establishes, and at the same time, accounts for the fact, that Satan was permitted to set up his oracles, in opposition to those of Jehovah. In perfect accordance with this, is the declaration of the apostle: 1 Cor. x. 20, "I say, that the things which the Gentiles sacrifice, they sacrifice to devils, (dæmons) and not to God, and I would not that ye should have fellowship with *devils*." Ye cannot drink the cup of the Lord, and the cup of devils; ye cannot be partakers of the Lord's table, and of the table of devils."

Satan also instituted an ephod, or *Teraphim*, in opposition to the Urim and Thummim of the High-priest of Jehovah. The idolatry of Micah described in Judges, xvii., establishes this. "The man Micah had a house of gods, and made an ephod, and teraphim, and consecrated one of his sons, who became his priest." The same passage proves also, that the very ordination to the priesthood was mimicked and counterfeited by Satan.

The portions of Scripture, however, which settle the question of Satanic influence upon the minds of those who turned aside from the service of God and became apostates and idolaters—the strongest and most unanswerable passages are those which relate to, and peremptorily forbid all communications with so called familiar spirits, and all consultations of persons who professed to have dealings with them. In the Old Testament writings, no less than sixteen passages occur, in which reference is made to this form of Satanic influence. In the Levitical law, it was expressly ordained, "A man also, or a woman, that hath a familiar spirit, or that is a wizard, shall surely be put to death; they shall stone them with stones; their blood shall be upon them." (Lev. 20–27.) The prohibition was also inserted in the statutes, and the reason was assigned in these words: "Regard not them that have familiar spirits, neither seek after wizards to be defiled by them; I am the Lord thy God." It is worthy of remark, that in all the passages which bear upon this subject, the communication with evil spirits is represented as *real;* the Scriptures do not speak, in a single instance, as though it was a mere pretence of impostors, and yet there can be no doubt, that many of the acts which were practised by the magicians, wizards, soothsayers, and sorcerers, were the merest tricks of juggling and legerdemain. With all this, however, there was besides, an actual direct and special communication with malignant dæmons, the emissaries of the devil, who gave responses and uttered predictions, which were sometimes verified, but were frequently proved false by subsequent events. In the description of Manasseh's character, (2 Chron. xxx. 6,) we read: "He observed times and used enchantments, and used witchcraft, and *dealt with a familiar spirit*, and with wizards." This language certainly implies more than mere pretence or profession; it represents Manasseh as actually dealing with a familiar spirit. The narrative of Saul's application to the "Witch of Endor," is strong and relevant testimony to the same effect. In this connection, we may properly remark, that not a single instance can be adduced in which the inspired writers speak with approbation, or even with allowance or toleration of those who dealt with familiar spirits, or used enchantments, or practised the arts of magic, or soothsaying, or fortune-telling. In all cases, the men of God, who spake as they were moved by the Holy Ghost, reprobate all such practices and denounce the conduct of those who use such arts, or who apply to those who practice them as flagrant offences and heinous sins in the sight of God. This is an important fact, because it plainly implies that the spirits who were consulted were angels or emissaries of the devil. No pure, no holy being would be found enticing men to transgress the commands of God. This whole subject derives additional importance from the theories which have recently been broached, and which are based upon alleged facts and discoveries and revelations from the spirit world, but I waive this topic for the present, as I purpose directing attention to it in a subsequent chapter. A single remark may suffice meanwhile, the truth of which will be obvious to every one who receives the Bible as the book from which there can be no appeal; it is this; no *new* revelation purporting to come from the spirit world can be of God, because that would be either adding to the sacred canon, or taking from it, and the great Head of the Church has declared, in the very last sentences of the revelation of his word, that there shall be no taking away from its statutes, and no adding to them till he come, and that they who presume to do either, do it at the peril of remediless damnation! Let these revelations, therefore, be what they may, either real communications made by dæmons, or the tricks of mountebanks or charlatans, they are alike all abominable. I do not say that they are positively unreal, for I find in the prophecies of the Revelation of St. John, that a period will come in the history of the Church, signalised by delusion, and that "spirits of devils," or dæmons, shall "go forth, working miracles," to gather the kings of the earth and the whole world to the battle of the great day of God Almighty; that time is even now; that day has come, robed in clouds of war, dark and boding terror and sorrow. It behoves us to be prepared for it, and to remember that whilst Satan cannot work real miracles, he can perform, and his angels also, "lying wonders," by which he might deceive, were it possible, *the very elect.*

In addition to those who dealt with familiar

spirits, the Scriptures speak of various kinds of magicians, soothsayers, diviners, necromancers, astrologers, wizards, sorcerers, &c., who were engaged in the exercise of arts of divination, or in the practice of imposture and juggling, intended to deceive and seduce the people of God from the worship of Jehovah. All these practices are forbidden, not only in the Old Testament, but also in the New, and therefore we are not to regard them as obsolete instrumentalities of the devil. They have not fallen into disuse; if they ever had, Satan has revived them in our day with a vigour and an impudence that deserve a stern rebuke. Some of the false prophets, already enumerated, were engaged in *casting nativities*, others in *fortune-telling*, others in communications with dæmons; but all, of whatever name or cast, were by statute law, proscribed in Israel, and were subject under the Jewish theocracy to the penalty of death.

The reason of this severity is plain. Jehovah was the political head and ruler of the Jewish nation, and as the ceremonial and moral law were blended under his government, they who enticed his covenant people into the abominations of idol-service and devil-worship, were guilty of high treason against the divine administration, and God set the seal of his abhorrence upon these abominations, by meting out to them the severest penalty of the civil law. The gospel brings eternal things into clearer view. It teaches men to look forward to the eternal state, upon whose borders they tarry for a little while, for the full measure of the retribution which awaits the wicked, and, therefore, the severity of the ceremonial law is not to be enforced in any case, unless it be reserved by express or implied stipulation in the New Testament; but let Christians remember this, that if astrologers and soothsayers, and fortune-tellers and sorcerers are not to be punished by human tribunals with death, they are not less abominable in the sight of God than they were under the ancient dispensation. One of the very last sentences in the Bible declares, that *sorcerers* are among the outcasts from heaven, who never shall enter the gates of the holy city. I would as soon think of visiting the purlieus of hell, as consulting the impudent impostors who pretend to foretell future events by their arts of infernal divination, and I cannot conceive a greater scandal to a Christian profession, or a sin more abominable in the sight of God, and more insulting to the Lord Jesus Christ, than for a professed follower of the Saviour to consult a vile fortune-teller or a caster of nativities, or one who professes to deal with a familiar spirit. This was the sin of

Saul, and for this very sin he was slain. Even when they speak the truth, they speak it through the agency of him who was a liar from the beginning, and who never says what is true, when a lie will better subserve his purpose. The folly of the thing, apart from its intense wickedness, should deter all persons of ordinary intelligence from practising it. Prescience, or foreknowledge, is not an attribute of Satan. He knows nothing beforehand, except what God has been pleased to reveal. The future belongs to God; it depends not upon the combinations of stars or planets; it is not to be read in the lines of a man's face, or in the palm of his hand, but it rests in the purpose and will of God. They who seek counsel of any but the Lord, do in that very act worship the god of this world. To consult a caster of nativities is to pray to the devil, and Satan has already a hold upon the hearts of men, strong enough and broad enough to effect their ruin without any pains on their part to make assurance doubly sure. You see this power illustrated in the terrible predominance which long indulgence will give to any vice or depraved habit, over the human mind, rendering its subject literally the captive of the devil. About five years ago, in a miserable garret, in the city of Cincinnati, a wretched woman, attended by an only daughter, a girl of some sixteen years, lay in the agony of death. For many years she had followed the trade of a street beggar, and had amassed a very considerable amount of money, which was secured in gold and silver coin, in a chest. She was a perfect slave of avarice, living in the most abject poverty apparently grudging herself the very necessaries of life, though obtained without any expenditure of her beloved treasure. From her daughter's statement, it appears, that she had not only trained her child to the same wretched vocation, but had been in the habit of beating her unmercifully whenever the daily proceeds of her business fell below a certain average. The miserable woman fell sick. The idea of calling in medical aid and being compelled to purchase the requisite medicines, was almost as terrible to her as death itself. She refused to do it. The disease ran its course, and she became aware that she must die. She had lost the power of motion, but not of speech, and she bade her daughter bring the key of her chest. "Put it into my hand," said she. "Now clench my fingers upon it." It was done. "Place this hand in my bosom;" and her daughter put aside the tattered garment and laid that clenched and clammy hand upon her mother's breast. "Now," she exclaimed, "draw my cot over towards the chest." Her daughter obeyed. "Lay this hand upon the lid." This too was done. And struggling as shê was with death, the wretched woman clung to her treasure, raving, that she would not give it up, and that she must take it with her. In that posture death found her, and when the spirit had fled, the hands of that ghastly corpse were still clutching the key and the lid of the miser's chest. She was a worshipper of "the god of this world;" her ruling passion strong in death, she died as she had lived, the slave of the devil.

How different is this from the close of a Christian's life. An eminent man of God lay upon his dying bed. The power of memory, owing to the nature of the disease, seemed almost extinct. Still there was consciousness His son approached him and whispered, "Father, do you know me?" "Who are you?" said the dying man. "I am your son." "My son! I do not remember that I ever had a son!" His wife, amid tears which almost choked her utterance, bent over him and asked, "Do you remember *me?*" "Who are *you?*" "I am your wife." He gazed vacantly upon her and shook his head, in token that he did not recognize even her. A friend stepped towards the bed, and taking his hand, inquired, "Do you know the Lord Jesus Christ?" "The Lord Jesus Christ!" he exclaimed, whilst a smile of intelligence kindled upon his countenance, "oh, yes! I have known him these many, many years." So, when all the ties of earth are sundered and memory has lost its hold upon the dearest affinities of this life, the child of God still clings to Christ—the first and the last—the Author of faith and its Finisher.

REVELATION XVI. 13.

"They are the spirits of (devils) dæmons working miracles."

CHAPTER V.

SATAN, THE DECEIVER.

THESE remarkable words occur in the symbolic vision of the sixth vial, and relate to events which are to precede the gathering together of the nations to the battle of that great day of God Almighty. The inspired apostle declares, that he beheld "three unclean spirits, like frogs, come out of the mouth of the dragon, and out of the mouth of the beast, and out of the mouth of the false prophet; for they are the spirits of devils," dæmon-spirits, "working miracles." The most commonly received interpretation of the vision is that which refers the three powers, which send forth the three unclean spirits like frogs, respectively, to the rulers of the Eastern Roman Empire, symbolized by the dragon, the rulers of the Western Roman Empire, symbolized by the wild beast, and to the ecclesiastical and civil rulers or hierarchy of the papal states, represented by the false prophet.

There is a singular unanimity in English commentaries in the application of one at least of these classes of unclean spirits, to the Jesuits.

The word "spirits" is sometimes used to denote religious teachings (in the language of Scripture). Thus, the apostle John says (1 Ep. iv. i.) "Beloved, believe not every spirit, but try the spirits whether they be of God, because many false prophets are gone out into the world." It is remarkable also, that in the primitive church, among the supernatural, or præternatural endowments, the gift of discerning spirits, is enumerated. This faculty enabled its possessor to judge infallibly, whether any one, who professed to be moved by the Holy Ghost, was really thus actuated, or under the influence of impure spirits. The interpretation by which these unclean spirits are represented as false teachers of religion, is supported by the analogy of Scripture. An old commentator on the Revelation, Thomas Brightman, whose book was published, A. D., 1616, uses this language in the explication of the passage before us. After stating that these emissaries, or unclean spirits are Jesuits, and that they are bound by their vow to go wherever the ecclesiastical authority shall send them, and on whatever errand their superior may prescribe, he says: "They are like unto frogs, because they delight in their own most filthy abominations of doctrine, out of which they fetch their beginning and their life. They refuse to be clothed with Christ's righteousness, boasting themselves of their own mire, as if they were clean enough therewith, to appear before God. And seeing the sea was made all like carrionly filthy blood before this, what other thing is there that can delight in so filthy a pool, where such weeds grow, but frogs, toads, and such kinds of execrable vermin, that came from the lake of fire and brimstone, and shall thither again, one day? But besides their filthiness, they are like frogs also in their importunate croaking. For, these bellows of troubles and war-making Furies shall leave nothing undone, that they may set the whole world in a combustion. But why is there no difference made between the captains and soldiers of the Pope and the Turks? Because, although nothing shall be more common in the Jesuits and Papists, than the name of Jesus Christ, so that they will be called *Jesuits*, from thence, yet seeing they hope for life and salvation by their own merits, they differ nothing from the heathens, who do wholly despise Christ." Whether this interpretation is authorized, or not, is not now the question with me. My design is not to speak about the Jesuits, but to view the words in their literal acceptation, as bearing upon the subject of Satanic influence and power. Nor, can it be any objection, that the language is metaphorical, for the terms of a metaphor must always indicate things which are in themselves real. For example, when we wish to predicate the qualities of boldness, or courage of a man, we may speak metaphorically, and say, "he is a Lion;" but there would be no meaning in such language, were it not admitted that the lion is bold and courageous. So, when we indicate meekness or gentleness, we sometimes say that such a person is a lamb; but the metaphor would be stripped of all its significance, if the lamb was not a type of these very qualities. So in the case before us, the idea of comparing false teachers to unclean spirits, or to dæmon spirits, working miracles, would be perfectly nugatory and absurd, were there no such beings as dæmons, possessing the power of working wonders. This analogy is perfectly plain, and the use of this passage, as authority in point, is manifestly legitimate. I have already stated, in a former chapter, that the Devil cannot work a true miracle. This power belongs to God alone. A miracle implies a suspension of the physical laws of God, and Satan would therefore possess the means of subverting the divine government, if this prerogative pertained to him. We must remember, however, that Satan has ability vastly superior to any that can be exercised by man. An effect may therefore be superhuman, and yet not miraculous. The Devil may do more than man can do, because he possesses superior knowledge and strength. He has facilities for understanding the laws of nature; he may be, and doubtless is, perfectly familiar with the natural causes of phenomena, the rationale of which is concealed from our view. He has studied them for six thousand years. Hence many things may appear to be miraculous to us, which are merely the proper results of natural causes. We have seen too, that the great Enemy has the faculty of deluding the minds and senses of men, so that he can make things appear other than they really are. Hence, the Scriptures speak of the "lying wonders" wrought by the power of the Devil. Thus the apostle Paul declared that at a certain period in the history of the Church, the man of sin should be revealed, that Wicked One the Son of Perdition, whose coming is after the working of Satan, with all power, and *signs* and LYING WONDERS, and with all deceivableness of unrighteousness in them that perish, and farther, that for the very reason, that his dupes should hate the truth and take pleasure in unrighteousness, God would send them strong delusion, withdraw the restraints of his grace, permit them who say to him "Depart from us, we desire not the knowledge of thy ways," to walk in their own counsels, "that they all might be damned who believed not the truth, but had pleasure in unrighteousness." This blindness, or delusion, is judicial; it is a punishment upon them who do violence to the dictates of their own consciences, and to the strivings of the Holy Ghost. It is the terrible precursor of damnation, wrought by the power of the Devil upon them who are led captive by him at his will. Let us, then, examine the testimony of the Scriptures and weight the evidence presented in the word of God, in support of this wonder-working faculty of dæmon spirits. We have already adverted to the practice of dealing with familiar spirits described and denounced in the Old Testament, and we find some traces of it in the New Testament also. The wizards or witches, spoken of in the Old Testament writers, were persons of this description; they are another name for those who dealt with familiar spirits. In the book of the Acts of the Apostles, we find several incidents bearing upon this point, to be noticed in due order, and the Apostle Paul in his Epistle to the Galatians, (v. 20,) enumerates "witchcraft" among the forbidden practices which are abominable in the sight of God, and of which he says, "I have told you in time past, that they which do such things shall not inherit the kingdom of God." It is a mistaken idea, therefore, that this is an obsolete sin, under the new dispensation, for if it were, the Apostle would not enumerate it among the crimes of idolatry, and adultery, and hatred, and heresies, and drunkenness, and murder, which are all rife in the world to this day.

The case, which will at once occur to the mind of every one who is familiar with the Scriptures, as an illustration of the subject before us, is the narrative of the Witch of Endor, recited in 1 Sam. xxviii. Saul had manifested great zeal against all who had dealings with familiar spirits; he "had put away those that had familiar spirits, and the wizards out of the land." Being sorely pressed and menaced by a formidable host of Philistines, the most inveterate enemies of Israel, "he was afraid, and his heart greatly trembled. And when Saul inquired of the Lord, the Lord answered him not, neither by dreams, nor by Urim, nor by prophets." Distressed by the silence of the divine oracles, which had hitherto always given responses, when duly consulted, and regarding the restraint which God had placed upon the ordained instrumentalities of special revelation, as a token of divine displeasure, Saul was agitated by the most fearful perplexity. Samuel, the man of God, who had so often stood in the breach before Jehovah, and had rescued the king and the people of Israel from the most imminent peril, by his fervent and faithful intercession, had gone to his rest.

"Samuel was dead, and all Israel had lamented him, and buried him in Ramah, even in his own city." The thought of Samuel was uppermost in the mind of Saul. He had been a true friend of the King; for though Saul had often been rebuked with all the severity of faithfulness, he had never been deceived by the prophet. And now, that the black clouds of impending wrath were again lowering over the land, and the oracles were silent, and there was no prophet like Samuel, to tell the king the counsel of the Lord, the bereavement with which God had afflicted the nation, in taking away his own faithful servant, added gall to the bitterness of Saul's perplexity. His conscience troubled him. God had forsaken him, and he knew the reason. How his heart trembled, when he looked from the camp of Israel in Gilboa, out towards Shunem, and saw it covered with the mighty array of the Philistines! How he groaned in the anguish of despair, Oh! that Samuel were with me! See him in his tent, bowing his face to the earth, whilst tears of vexation course down his cheeks, and he moans in broken sentences, his sad complaint, that God has departed from him, and repeats with passionate earnestness, the name of the revered prophet, Samuel! Samuel! Suddenly a suggestion has darted into his mind. It is a fiery arrow of the Wicked One. He repels it. The subtle Tempter pleads; Saul listens. *What wilt thou do? There is no prophet like* SAMUEL, *to prevail with God in an hour like this. Thy prophets are dumb. There is no vision from the Lord in all Israel. The Urim and Thummim upon the breast of the high priest has lost its virtue. God will not hear thee; but, peradventure there is* ANOTHER *who can befriend thee! Seek one who has a familiar spirit; thou mayest yet see Samuel!* We may well conceive, that it must have cost the king a severe struggle before he could yield to this temptation. He had driven the necromancers out of the land by the severest penalties, and if any ventured still to practise their forbidden arts, they were compelled to skulk in the caves of the earth, through fear of Saul's vengeance. He yields at length, and his resolution is taken. "Then said Saul unto his servants, Seek me a woman that hath a familiar spirit, that I may go to her, and inquire of her. And his servants said to him, Behold, there is a woman that hath a familiar spirit at En-dor. And Saul disguised himself, and put on other raiment, and he went, and two men with him, and they came to the woman by night: and he said, I pray thee, divine unto me by the familiar spirit, and bring me him up, whom I shall name unto thee. And the woman said unto him, Behold, thou knowest what Saul hath done, how he hath cut off those that have familiar spirits, and the wizards, out of the land; wherefore then layest thou a snare for my life, to cause me to die? And Saul sware to her by the Lord, saying, As the Lord liveth, there shall no punishment happen to thee for this thing. Then said the woman, Whom shall I bring up unto thee? And he said, Bring me up Samuel. And when the woman saw Samuel, she cried with a loud voice: and the woman spake to Saul, saying, Why hast thou deceived me? for thou art Saul. And the king said unto her, Be not afraid; for what sawest thou? And the woman said unto Saul, I saw gods ascending out of the earth. And he said unto her, What form is he of? And she said, An old man cometh up; and he is covered with a mantle. And Saul perceived that it was Samuel, and he stooped with his face to the ground, and bowed himself. And Samuel said to Saul, Why hast thou disquieted me, to bring me up? And Saul answered, I am sore distressed; for the Philistines make war against me, and God is departed from me, and answereth me no more, neither by prophets, nor by dreams; therefore I have called thee, that thou mayest make known unto me what I shall do. Then said Samuel, Wherefore then dost thou ask of me, seeing the Lord is departed from thee, and is become thine enemy? And the Lord hath done to him, as he spake by me: for the Lord hath rent the kingdom out of thine hand, and given it to thy neighbor, even to David: Because thou obeyedst not the voice of the Lord, nor executedst his fierce wrath upon Amalek, therefore hath the Lord done this thing unto thee this day. Moreover the Lord will also deliver Israel with thee into the hand of the Philistines: and to-morrow shalt thou and thy sons be with me; the Lord also shall deliver the host of Israel into the hand of the Philistines. Then Saul fell straightway all along the earth, and was sore afraid, because of the words of Samuel: and there was no strength in him; for he had eaten no bread all the day, nor all the night." This history teaches certain important practical truths, with which we are mainly concerned at present.

Those who followed the profession of the woman of Endor, had dealings with, or communications from departed spirits, or dæmons. She had at her command a dæmon which could inquire of the departed spirits, and give information. Sometimes the information was true, at other times it may have been false, according to the purpose which Satan intended to accomplish. To adopt the theory, that these communication were *never* real, is to involve the plainest declarations of Scripture in contradiction and absurdity. In fact, there is not a single passage in the whole Bible which represents these dealings with dæmon-spirits as mere pretence, and yet there can be no doubt that many of the wonders which were wrought professedly by demoniacal instrumentality were nothing more than tricks of juggling charlatans.

It is altogether probable that the woman whom Saul consulted at Endor, recognized the king through his disguise, at the very moment when he entered her dwelling. The camp of Israel was not very far from Endor, and the stature of Saul was such, and his personal appearance was so well known, that it would be difficult for him to elude detection in any disguise. Then his embarrassment, the distress, amounting almost to despair, by which he was agitated, would all tend to betray him. This opinion is moreover confirmed by the conduct of the woman herself. When requested to bring up the one whom Saul should name, she replies: "Behold, thou knowest what Saul hath done, how he hath cut off those that have familiar spirits, and the wizards out of the land; wherefore then layest thou a snare for my life, to cause me to die? And Saul sware to her by the Lord, saying, as the Lord liveth, there shall no punishment happen to thee for this thing." Now, would the woman have been satisfied with such a promise, even though confirmed by an oath, unless she had known that the person who made it was able to protect her? She is ready to proceed so soon as she has the oath of Saul as her guarantee, but she keeps her discovery to herself, until it suits her purpose to inform the king that his disguise is unnecessary. This deceit on the part of the woman is in perfect accordance with the character of one who dealt habitually with a wicked spirit; still I cannot adopt the theory, that the whole scene in which Samuel is introduced was the mere effect of imposture, for the following reasons. *The Scripture narrative describes it as real.* There is not a word in the entire account which expresses a doubt in the mind of the inspired writers respecting its reality. Had the whole matter been a mere trick, would it not have been exposed by the man of God who wrote the book of Samuel? Would he, moved as he was by the Spirit of truth, have recorded the story in such a manner as to make a false impression upon the mind of the reader? Take, for instance, a single passage, "Saul perceived that it was Samuel, and he stooped with his face to the ground and bowed himself. And *Samuel* said to Saul, why hast thou disquieted me to bring me up?" Evidently it was the honest conviction of the inspired writer, that Samuel was sent to give the terrible message which the apparition addressed to the King of Israel. Again, the prediction of the spirit was verified by the event. He tells Saul, "the Lord will also deliver Israel with thee into the hand of the Philistines, and to-morrow shalt thou and thy sons be with me!" In the thirty-first chapter of 1 Samuel, the narrative confirms the prophecy, for "the Philistines fought against Israel: and the men of Israel fled from before the Philistines, and fell down slain in Mount Gilboa, and the Philistines followed hard upon Saul and his sons; and they slew Jonathan, and Abinadab and Melchishua, Saul's sons. And the battle went sore against Saul, and the archers hit him; and he was sore wounded of the archers. Then said Saul unto his armour-bearer, Draw thy sword and thrust me through therewith; but his armour-bearer would not: for he was sore afraid. Therefore Saul took a sword and fell upon it. And when his armour-bearer saw that Saul was dead, he fell likewise upon his sword, and died with him. So Saul died, and his three sons, and his armour-bearer, and all his men, that same day together." (Ch. xxxi. 6.) Now, if we assume that Satan personated Samuel, as some pretend, how shall we account for the literal fulfilment of these minute details of the spectre's prophecy? Foreknowledge, or prescience, is not of Satan. He may guess, but he can know nothing beforehand, except what God has revealed. And will God send the Spirit of Truth to enable the Devil to prophesy? If so, there would indeed have been some good reason for consulting one who had a familiar spirit. No. It was Samuel who spoke to Saul. The Scriptures would not tell us that *Samuel* addressed the king, if they meant that *Satan* was the speaker. God permitted the soul of the prophet to return, and from the borders of the eternal world to utter a terrible confirmation of the truth which he had spoken, while living on the earth. Some have argued, that if Samuel had been present, he would have urged Saul to repentance, and that the absence of any such admonition is proof that Satan was personating the prophet and seeking to drive the wretched monarch to despair. To this, we answer, that in no single instance, in which God has given a man up to walk in his own counsels, is the abandonment associated with the call to repentance. Elijah declared to king Ahaziah, that he should surely die, when the king had sent messengers to consult Baalzebub, the god of Ekron, but he gave him no call to repent. Daniel foretold to Belshazzar, his impending doom, but he made no offer of mercy, and Samuel predicted the discomfiture of Israel and the death of Saul and his sons, but he said not a word to Saul to open the way of pardon, because *God had departed from him.* "Yea, woe also unto them, when I shall depart from them," saith the Lord. "Ephraim is joined to idols; let him alone." Let it be remembered, that two out of the three instances of utter judicial abandonment, above cited, were punishments entailed upon kings who forsook the oracles of Jehovah, and went to consult emissaries of Satan, who were in league with hell; and the third was a Pagan king, who polluted the vessels of the Lord's house by a drunken revel in honour of his Babylonish idols. Sacrilege and blasphemy are evident tokens of perdition; they are the dark harbingers of hell!

Many reflections, suggested by this narrative, must be passed by, but we will briefly notice two points which are among the most important in their practical bearing. The prophet Samuel complains, when he comes up before Saul, "Why hast *thou* disquieted me to bring me up?" He seems to intimate by this rebuke, that he was there not because he was subject to the magic incantations of the woman of Endor, but by the special direction of God. He takes no notice of her, either by speaking of her, or by speaking to her. Again he complains that Saul has *disquieted* him. It was bringing him back to mingle in grief with which he was to be no more acquainted. Shall he leave the Paradise of God to listen again to the recital of human woes, and have his kind heart harrowed by the sight of Saul's despair? "Why hast *thou disquieted* me?" A legitimate inference from this passage, would seen to teach, that those dæmons who hold communication with necromancers, are wicked spirits. Indeed, as we have already remarked, this follows plainly from the statutes, prohibiting the arts of necromancy. No holy spirit would be accessory to the transgression of God's law. Moses and Elias appeared on Tabor, but they appeared in glory; they visited Christ when he was transfigured; they came to speak with him of the decease he was shortly to accomplish at Jerusalem.

Another point is this. Samuel declares to Saul, "To-morrow shalt thou, with thy sons, be with me." This is to be understood as a prediction that they would be with Samuel in the spirit world, precisely as we might say of two men, of opposite moral and religious character, that after death, they are both in the eternal world; though one may be in Paradise and the other in Tartarus, one, like Lazarus in Abraham's bosom in heaven, the other groaning with Dives in hell, yet both are in Hades—that word denoting merely the state of departed spirits in general, the intermediate state of the soul, between the death and resurrection of the body, without reference to the particular habitation of the righteous and the wicked. This is the true meaning of Hades, and it is plain, that it is not to be rendered, as it sometimes is in our version, by the word hell, because it includes both heaven and hell—the abodes both of the saved and of the lost. We proceed now to the farther investigation of the subject properly before us. In the New Testament, we find incidental allusions to this form of Satanic influence. In the book of Acts, (xix. 13,) where the success of the gospel at Ephesus is narrated, we read after the statement that many who believed came and confessed their deeds, "Many of them also which used curious arts, brought their books together, and burned them before all men, and they counted the price of them, and found it fifty thousand pieces of silver. So mightily grew the word of God and prevailed." This immense price shows the number of books consumed to have been great, and proves that the extent to which these forbidden practices were carried was, by no means, inconsiderable in the apostolic age. When Paul was at Thyatira, a damsel who had a spirit of divination and brought her masters much gain by soothsaying, followed the apostle and his coadjutors in the gospel, saying, These men are the servants of the Most High God, which show unto us the way of salvation. The apostle commanded the spirit in the name of the Lord Jesus to come out of her; and he came out, and with that departure the hope of her masters' gains departed also. (Acts xvi. 16–18.) This incident affords positive proof that the divinations of some soothsayers, are not always mere human impostures, but are sometimes the effect of real Satanic operations. Had the divination here described been simply a juggling collusion between the damsel and her masters, the apostle would not have ascribed it to the agency of an evil spirit, and the terms of the narrative and its whole character would have been changed. In connection with this passage, we would refer you to the words in Deut. xiii. 16. "If there arise among you a prophet, or a dreamer of dreams, and giveth thee a sign or a wonder, and the sign or the wonder come to pass, whereof he spake unto thee, saying, Let us go after other gods, which thou hast not known, and let us serve them; thou shalt not hearken unto the words of that prophet, or that dreamer of dreams; for the Lord your God proveth you, to know whether ye love the Lord your God with all your heart and with all your soul. Ye shall walk after the Lord your God, and fear him and keep his commandments, and obey his voice, and ye shall serve him, and cleave unto him. And that prophet, or that dreamer of dreams, shall be put to death; because he hath spoken to turn you away from the Lord your God," &c. This confirms our position, and proves beyond all controversy, that Satan did both under the old and new dispensations exercise a direct and special influence upon the minds of his subjects, and that by his conjectural knowledge, and more than human foresight, he was permitted to make wonderful discoveries through the human agents who were under his control. Now, I can not only find no passage in the Scriptures, in support of the commonly received idea which limits this Satanic agency to ancient periods in the history of the world, or of the Church, but I believe also, that passages may be adduced which will establish the very opposite. The words announced as my topic, "Spirits of dæmons working miracles," occur in the prophetic history of the events of the sixth vial, which relate in regular order to the latest period but one in the history of the Church; the seventh vial is the period immediately preceding the millennial kingdom. That era will be signalized by a great increase of Satanic power. The hosts of darkness will be permitted, as it were, to break down some of the barriers by which they have hitherto been restrained, and it is generally admitted, not only that we are rapidly approaching this great crisis in the experience of the Church of Christ, but that it has already begun. "Behold," says the Master, "I come as a thief! Blessed is he that watcheth and keepeth his garments." (v. 15.)

Why should one of the last warnings recorded in the book of God relate to "sorcerers," if the crime of which they are guilty was so soon to be an obsolete offence? Besides, if we examine the testimony of history, if we even go no farther back than our own day, we shall find proof enough of the lying, wonder-working power of dæmon spirits.

About two hundred years ago, the popular belief on the subject of dæmon influence was tainted with the darkest fanaticism, and there can be no doubt, that many innocent persons were put to a cruel death on false accusations of practising arts of witchcraft. This is admitted by all who are at pains to examine the record of these transactions. Effects which are now clearly understood to be the results of natural causes, were, in that age, ascribed to the devil's agency. Ventriloquism, for instance, which is manifestly a natural faculty in some persons, produced by a peculiar structure or exercise of the organs of speech, was at one time, regarded as unequivocal proof of witchcraft. This mistake originated in the well-known fact, that the ancient necromancers frequently employed ventriloquism to deceive those who came to consult them. So, again, effects were ascribed to the power of witchcraft, which were nothing more than the natural and necessary results of certain forms of disease; but whilst making all these allowances, I am by no means persuaded that the accusations were groundless in every instance, though I do not wish to be understood as advocating the Levitical severity with which both the innocent and the guilty have been punished. I believe, however, that the fact that multitudes in that age were really engaged in the ancient crime of dealing with familiar spirits, (a synonym for witchcraft,) is as clearly made out as any event ever was, or ever can be, and the testimony on this point is so cumulative and overwhelming, that no evidence of any fact or event can be worthy of belief, if this may be rejected. I shall quote but a single author, who, however, cites many authorities, and whom I regard as a host in himself, I mean the learned and excellent Richard Baxter. Although he falls into mistakes, common in that age, and adduces instances of supposed demoniacal influence, which were not necessarily, or even probably such in reality, it would be absurd, on this account, to reject other evidence, which is open to no such objection. Now Baxter states substantially, that in some eight or nine hundred cases which were adjudicated on the continent of Europe, in France, in Germany, in Savoy, in Italy, and also in great Britain, certain leading principles were observable throughout, and as he justly remarks, the circumstances were such as absolutely to preclude all possibility of collusion; because apart from the want of motive, the persons implicated were strangers to one another. It certainly is a strong fact, that all alike confessed that they did enter into covenant with Satan, that they renounced God and Christ and their baptism, and all communion with the Church, and that they had direct and special communications with evil spirits; that they had the faculty of associating with these dæmons at pleasure by means of arts which savour strongly of mesmerism, and that they were endowed by these familiar spirits with præter-human powers, which were employed for purposes of malice, mischief, or revenge. I will admit, that it is possible for the human mind to be so affected with morbid fanaticism, as to sink into a form of gloomy insanity, and that an excited and perverted imagination may, by preying upon itself, reduce the wretched victim of mental disease to a condition of hopeless and absolute delusion; such cases of confirmed lunacy are still to be found, but it would be difficult to reconcile the facts in Baxter's narrative with the phenomena invariably presented in this variety of insanity. I will let Baxter sum up his testimony in his own words. After stating, that notwithstanding all the authorities he has adduced, the reality of this form of Satanic influence was denied by many in his day, he uses this language: "If the testimonies of judges, justices, lawyers and juries, that have examined and heard the witnesses, and are themselves as tender of wrongfully putting people to death, as these infidels are; if the confessions of so many hundred witches at the halter or fire be not sufficient; if the records of so many judicatures be not sufficient; if men of so great piety, honesty, judgment and impartiality may not be credited in a case which bringeth no gain to themselves; if the testimony of so many several nations as France, Lorraine, Germany, Italy, be not sufficient; if the experience of all countries in the world, and all ages, who have found that same sort of wretched persons, be not sufficient; and, lastly, if the fresh experience of so many scores in a narrow compass at once imprisoned and put to death in our country, attested by so many thousand competent witnesses, and the frequent experiences of the judges in their circuits, be none of them sufficient to convince these infidels, I shall leave it either to God's grace or the devil's torments ere long to convince them." (Baxter's Works, Vol. II., p. 335. London, George Virtue, 1845.) This is strong language, and though great allowance must be made on account of the prevalent public opinion of the age, still it seems impossible, that *all* this elaborate detail adduced by him should have been altogether delusive, nor can I see, taking the Scriptures as our guide, any reason to doubt, that there were persons in his day, who had dealings with familiar spirits. I might cite similar testimony from the writings of John Wesley, and others, but I deem it superfluous. In our own day, the matter has been revived in a somewhat different form. If I am asked, do you believe all those stories that are told respecting the mysterious utterances and sounds and apparitions which are circulated in pamphlets and in the public prints? I answer, I will not believe any thing that is contrary to the Scriptures; I believe nothing without evidence that is indisputable. When persons of the highest veracity in all stations in society, who have been prejudiced against receiving any of these extraordinary phenomena, tell me what they themselves have witnessed, I cannot say, *I doubt your statements, and I do not believe you.* And when the word of God declares, that Satan shall come down in great wrath, knowing that his time is short, and that dæmon spirits shall go forth, working lying-wonders; and when I find that the tendency of all these *new revelations* is to impair and openly to subvert the sacred truths of the Bible, I feel that I am safe in saying to every Christian man and woman within the reach of my public or private influence, beware how you tamper with any of these arts—be they real or delusive—true or false—effects of dæmon power or of human fraud, they are alike of the devil, and the father of lies is their author. Beloved, it is the last time. Believe not every spirit, but try the spirits whether they be of God, for many false prophets are gone out into the world.

REVELATION IX. 11.

And they had a king over them which is the angel of the bottomless pit, whose name in the Hebrew tongue is Abaddon, but in the Greek tongue hath his name Apollyon.

CHAPTER VI.

SATAN, THE DESTROYER.

THE meaning of ABADDON and Apollyon, is Destroyer, and the appellation applies to the Angel of the bottomless pit, who is Satan, the prince of hell. The connection in which the words occur appears to me to be a conclusive demonstration of this interpretation. Some commentators, among whom Scott is pre-eminent, apply the symbolic prediction, in the course of which this passage occurs, to the rise and progress of Mohammed and his successors, who ruled over the Arabians and Saracens. In order to appreciate the force of this theory, it will be necessary to recite the entire vision, as recorded from the first to the twelfth verse of this chapter. "And the fifth angel sounded, and I saw a star fall from heaven unto the earth: and to him was given the key of the bottomless pit. And he opened the bottomless pit; and there arose a smoke out of the pit, as the smoke of a great furnace; and the sun and the air were darkened by reason of the smoke of the pit. And there came out of the smoke locusts upon the earth: and unto them was given power, as the scorpions of the earth have power. And it was commanded them that they should not hurt the grass of the earth, neither any green thing, neither any tree; but only those men which have not the seal of God in their foreheads. And to them it was given that they should not kill them, but that they should be tormented five months: and their torment *was* as the torment of a scorpion, when he striketh a man. And in those days shall men seek death, and shall not find it; and shall desire to die, and death shall flee from them. And the shapes of the locusts *were* like unto horses prepared unto battle; and on their heads *were* as it were crowns like gold, and their faces *were* as the faces of men. And they had hair as the hair of women, and their teeth were as *the teeth* of lions. And they had breast-plates, as it were breast-plates of iron; and the sound of their wings *was* as the sound of chariots of many horses running to battle. And they had tails like unto scorpions, and there were stings in their tails: and their power *was* to hurt men five months. And they had a king over them, *which is* the angel of the bottomless pit, whose name in the Hebrew tongue *is* Abaddon, but in the Greek tongue hath *his* name Apollyon. One wo is past; *and*, behold, there come two woes more hereafter." (Rev. ix. 1–12.) The star falling from heaven, according to this theory, is Mohammed; and the "bottomless pit" is the abyss of ruin into which his pestiferous doctrines, symbolized by the "great smoke," involves his followers. "The locusts" are the Saracens. The prohibition against destroying the fruits of the earth, and the permission to hurt those only who had not "the seal of God in their foreheads," is supposed to refer to, and to find its fulfilment in the fact, that the Saracens were forbidden to devastate the countries through which they passed, and that they made war only against the anti-christian powers who lent their aid to the apostate Church of Rome, typified by the "men, which have not the seal of God in their foreheads." The "torment" with which their victims were afflicted, is verified, according to this theory, in the calamities with which the Greek and Latin churches were oppressed, and the time, "five months," in prophetic language, every day symbolizing a year, indicates a period of one hundred and fifty years. Mohammed began his imposture, A. D. 612, and in 762, just one hundred and fifty years afterwards, the Saracens built Bagdad, and became a settled people, and made no more rapid conquests. The chief force of the Arabians consisted in their cavalry, indicated by the "horses prepared unto battle." The "crowns of gold on the head," denote either the "turban," which is the head-dress of the Arabs, or they may contain an allusion to the many kingdoms conquered by them. The "faces like men," and hair "as the hair of women," are understood to indicate the custom of the Arabs, who wore their hair plaited, or flowing loosely upon their shoulders. The "breast-plates of iron" may denote either their defensive armour, or their effective public measures. The "sound of their wings," prefigures the fury with which they assailed their enemies, and the "sting" in the scorpion tail, is a symbol of the deadly effect of their abominable religion. This is in a condensed form, the view of Scott, and of others who have adopted his theory of interpretation. It is certainly ingenious; in some points, it is very forcible; and throughout, at first sight, it is plausible, but I cannot adopt it as he presents it. The weak point in his theory is that which makes the "falling star," a symbol of Mohammed. The figure of a star is not unfrequently employed in the Apocalypse, as the symbol of a teacher of religion, but when applied to a promulgator of false doctrine, it always denotes an apostate, or one who originally professed the truth, and subsequently fell away from it. Now Mohammed, though a false teacher and a foul impostor, was not an apostate. The holy angels are spoken of in the book of Job as "the morning stars," who sang together, and the sons of God, who shouted for joy on the birth-day of creation. Satan is called Lucifer, or "the morning star." (Is. xiv. 12.) Thus, the prophet Isaiah exclaims, in allusion to Satan's expulsion from the abode of glory, "How art thou fallen from heaven, O Lucifer, son of the morning!" Does not our Saviour also say, "I saw Satan fall like lightning from heaven?" And was not the result of the war in heaven this, when Michael fought and his angels and the dragon fought and his angels, that no place was found for Satan any more in heaven, but the old serpent, called the Devil and Satan, was cast out into the earth, and his angels were cast out with him? (Rev. xii. 7, 8, 9.) With these collateral proofs secured in our minds, what will be the first thought on reading the announcement in the symbolic vision before us; "I saw a star fall from heaven unto the earth, and to him was given the key of the bottomless pit?" Will not the natural conclusion be, the whole analogy of Scripture declares "this star falling" from heaven unto the earth, designates plainly Satan, the leader of the apostate angels, who is the king of the bottomless pit? This is literally true of Satan; it is not true in any sense of Mohammed. Now put upon this cumulative testimony another weight, and I regard the demonstration as overwhelming. A Hebrew name is given to this angel of the bottomless pit. Why? Surely to indicate that he was the Destroyer, known to the Jews as Abaddon, the very title employed in the Old Testament as an appellation of Satan. Thus David says, "By the word of thy lips, I have kept me from the paths of the Destroyer." The star falling from heaven to the earth, the king who reigns over the bottomless pit, the angel who holds its key, whose name in Hebrew is Abaddon, and in Greek Apollyon, is not Mohammed, or the Caliphs, his successors, but SATAN, the Destroyer. As for the rest, the application of this vision to the Saracenic inroads is the most consistent of any that is advanced. Henry applies it to the Papacy, but this explanation does not accord with the symbols employed by the inspired writer, and cannot be maintained on the ground of conformity to the laws established by the Scriptures as the rule of interpretation. The portions of the Apocalypse which point to the Papal Church and State, are so plain that they admit of no reasonable doubt, and we should guard against indiscriminate, and forced explanations, lest we impair confidence in those interpretations, the consistency and relevancy of which are obvious and indubitable.

In his character as THE DESTROYER, we propose therefore to regard Satan, at present. This is his real and ultimate character. He is the Tempter, the Tyrant, the god of this world, the Deceiver, that he may be THE DESTROYER. He was a liar from the beginning, that he might be a murderer. He goeth about as a roaring lion, seeking whom he may devour. He tempts men to murmur and rebel against God, as he tempted the Jews of old, that he may betray them to their ruin. Hence, the apostle warns the Church of Corinth: "Neither murmur ye, as some of them also murmured, and were destroyed of the destroyer." He blinds the minds of men, and hardens their hearts by strong delusions, that they may believe a lie and be damned. The wrath of Satan is directed to the twofold object of rendering the lives of men miserable upon earth, and of blasting their hope and prospect of eternal life in heaven. When he cannot lure their feet from the path of God's testimonies, when despite of all his artifices they hold fast the truths of the gospel, he stirs up the passions of the wicked in whom he rules, and who hate the oracles of God, because they have pleasure in unrighteousness, and thus he has originated the fearful and long-continued persecutions of the Church, by which the saints of the living God, in all ages, since the death of Christ, have been worn out. The surest mode by which the devil can secure the temporal and everlasting misery of men, is by luring them from their allegiance to the commands of God. Thus he prevailed against the old world. The way of men became so corrupt upon the earth, that it was filled with violence. The foulest crimes were committed every where, without compunction or remorse, and men were taught to sneer at the warnings of the preacher of righteousness, in sight of the very ark which Noah was preparing as a refuge for his family. Lulled into false security by the deceitfulness of sin, their hearts were utterly hardened against all truth; they mocked at fear, waxing bolder in sin as their destruction became more imminent, and whilst the darkening heavens and the muttering thunder were sending out the last warning of heaven, they continued scoffing at the threatened deluge, whilst the destroyer held a jubilee in the bottomless pit, and flung wide open the gates of hell to receive the children of perdition; and, when at last, the fountains of the great deep were broken up, and the ocean billows, dislodged from their accustomed bed, were poured upon the dry land, and the descending rain and the fires and thunder of the bursting heavens, proclaimed the advent of the day of wrath, Satan and his apostate legions revelled in the wide-spread ruin which the wickedness of men and the temptations and delusions of the destroyer had consummated. Then hell reaped her first great harvest, and from that day the flood has been the type of the great day when the Son of man shall come in the clouds, and the Lord Jesus shall be revealed in flaming fire, taking vengeance on them that know not God, and that obey not the gospel.

The next great trophy in the path of "the Destroyer" is seen in the fiery tempest which consumed Sodom and Gomorrah, and the cities of the plain. The wicked inhabitants of those purlieus of the pit, heeded not the voice of Lot. They vexed his righteous spirit. Given up to the vilest abominations, they set God at defiance. The Destroyer established his strongholds in the midst of their streets. They worshipped at his shrine, until the outraged patience of Heaven would no longer bear their provocations. God overthrew those cities with fire from heaven, and the smoke of the smouldering ruins went up as the smoke of a great furnace. Then, that the very ground, accursed of God, might forever be hidden from the sunlight and the sight of men, the Lord covered it with the waters of the

Dead Sea. We trace the progress of the Destroyer in the wicked rebellious spirit in which Pharaoh resisted the commands of God. But for the delusions of Satan, the king of Egypt might have consented to let Israel depart in peace, but at every symptom of relenting, the Destroyer stirred up the pride and passion of Pharaoh, and though his kingdom and his house were made desolate by the scourging plagues, still Satan ruled. If Moses and Aaron wrought miracles in proof of their authority as the messengers of God, the priests of Satan, the magicians, counterfeited them by lying wonders; thus, step by step, beckoning his victims onward to the borders of the Red Sea, leading them forth upon the track, which the hand of God had opened for the passage of his own people, the Destroyer triumphed in the destruction of Pharaoh and his host, and the exulting shouts of Abaddon and his legions mocked the terror and dismay of strong men in their agony, when weary with buffeting the returning waves, they sank like lead to the lowest depths. See, how he prevailed against the covenant people of God! What calamities overwhelmed them when they rebelled against Jehovah, seduced by the devices of the devil! They murmured for bread. Strange ingratitude! God fed them with manna from heaven, and man did eat angel's food, and yet they murmured still, "Our soul loatheth this light food!" The enemy did this. He enticed them to rebellion, that he might destroy them. God sent them flesh to eat, and the pestilence came with it. Read the record of Israel's experience in the wilderness, and see how the malice of Satan was continually exercised in exciting the pride and the unbelief and lusts of the Jews, that he might effect the ruin of the rebellious people. Look at the three thousand who were slain for their idolatry when Moses was on the mount with Jehovah. See the multitudes that perished in the rebellion of Korah, Dathan and Abiram, and the fourteen thousand and seven hundred that died of the plague, whilst the ground was still heaving in the convulsions of the terrible earthquake, in which the gainsayers had been swallowed up. See the camp covered with the dying people, bitten by fiery serpents—and again, behold the plagues bursting forth when the Hebrews joined themselves to Baal-peor, transgressing that command, "Ye shall no more offer your sacrifices unto dæmons," (Lev. xvii. 7,) and raging until twenty and four thousand had been destroyed. See how Satan tempted David to number Israel, that in the pride of his heart the king might trust in horses and chariots and armies, and forget that the name of the God of Jacob had ever been the great defence of his people. In all the calamities entailed upon the house of Israel by their repeated backslidings and apostacies from God, you behold the traces of Satan's power and malice as "the Destroyer." He inflames men to the utmost pitch of blasphemy against God, in the hope that they may be suddenly cut off and driven away in their wickedness. Nor has he prevailed only to the destruction of the souls and bodies of the wicked, who set at nought the law of God. All the cruelties which were inflicted under the old covenant by ungodly kings and rulers upon the prophets and people of God, were wrought by the agency of the Destroyer. Thus Jezebel, who slew the prophets of the Lord, and installed the priests of Baal, who offered sacrifice to dæmons, in the high places of Israel, is a type of the apostate Church under the new covenant, which has ever gloried in shedding the blood of the saints and of the martyrs of Jesus. The holy men of God, of whom St. Paul speaks, who wandered in the wilderness, seeking shelter in the dens and caves of the earth, were driven from the abodes of men, through the cruelty and malice of the Destroyer. You ask, as you see the earth covered with the bleaching bones of this vast multitude, some perishing under the indignation of heaven, others dying for the love they bore to the testimonies of God, Who hath slain all these? And the answer which the book of God gives is summed up in this—Abaddon the Destroyer is the murderer! He has made this earth an Aceldama, a field of blood; he has changed the terrestrial garden which was first a Paradise, into a Golgotha.

The Hebrews, and all the nations of the earth, before the coming of the Messiah, felt his power as Abaddon, the DESTROYER. But he has another name, APOLLYON, in the Greek tongue. He is the destroyer still. He had the power of death under the old covenant, and though Christ Jesus by his assumption of humanity and his triumph over death, has given to his believing people the glorious pledge of their final victory over all the powers of darkness, still Satan is Apollyon, the destroyer. Our blessed Lord was nailed to the cross through the power of the prince of darkness. True, he was a willing victim. He laid down his life freely. He had power to lay down his life and he had power to take it again; nevertheless, it was Satan who filled the hearts of the chief priests and rulers with hellish spite against the Saviour of men. Jesus went about doing good, dispensing gladness and mercy to the poor, healing the sick, casting out dæmons, and making every step of his path upon earth radiant with goodness, but for this very reason the children of the devil hated him. Satan entered into Judas and prevailed upon the traitor to betray his Master, for thirty pieces of silver; and when the treachery was complete, the tempter appears as the destroyer, urging the wretched apostate to go out and hang himself that he might go to his own place. In Gethsemane, Satan rolled the horror of great darkness upon the soul of Jesus, making him sorrowful even unto death, pressing him with the floods of hellish wrath, until his sweat was as it were great drops of blood falling down to the ground. How he groaned in the agony of his spirit, "Father, if it be possible, let this cup pass from me." When that ruthless band, led on by the traitor Judas, came upon him in the garden, he said, as he suffered them to lead him away, "This is your hour and the power of darkness." Oh! when Apollyon beheld Jesus nailed to the cross, when he saw the rabble exulting in the death of the Lamb of God, wagging their heads in derision, and taunting the Saviour with the bitter cry, "he saved others, himself he cannot save," when he gazed upon the changing countenance of the expiring Messiah, the fiendish joy of the dæmons of the pit filled every cavern of hell with howls of exultation and triumph. It was Apollyon who stirred up the rage of the cruel rabble; it was he who hardened the heart of the murderous throng, quenching every spark of human sympathy and pity; it was he who steeled and seared their conscience, making it proof against every pang of compunction! That was truly the hour of the power of darkness! The gates of hell had moved from beneath, and the angel of the bottomless pit stood upon this world, as the victorious destroyer. But the triumph was short-lived. The morning of the third day dawned, and angels came down to hail the awaking Saviour. The astonished keepers fell back and became as dead men. The dæmons who stood around that sepulchre fled with terror before the face of the rising Redeemer. Jesus came forth the conqueror of death, and the terrors of the grave were all dispelled. The Destroyer beheld in that victory the earnest of his own destruction. The fiery dart which had been aimed at Jesus, rebounded from the sepulchre and pierced the great adversary, and the shout of exultation was changed into a cry of savage disappointment and despair. Jesus was risen and ascended, and Jesus and the resurrection became the theme of the apostles and prophets of the new covenant. The gospel news of salvation through the crucified and risen Saviour ran and was glorified. Thousands flocked to the standard of the Man of Calvary. Heathen temples were forsaken; Satan's altars were cast down. His idols were broken; and the ruins of his power were scattered like trophies over the pathway of the heralds of the cross. He stirred up Jews and Gentiles to blaspheme and persecute. They shed the blood of Stephen; they slew the apostles; they cast the followers of Jesus into prison; they thrust the Christians into their amphitheatres to be devoured by wild beasts; they chained the martyrs to stakes and burned them; they tore their flesh piecemeal with knives and pincers, and the Destroyer revelled in the slaughter of the saints; but still the preachers of the great salvation testified of Jesus; the blood of the martyrs became the seed of the church; their sound went out into all the world, and the ends of the earth heard the name of Christ and rejoiced in it. Whole nations received the Gospel, and the empire of the Destroyer was shaken to its centre; it began to totter towards its fall. There was joy in heaven over myriads of repenting sinners. There was joy on earth, for ten thousand thousand saints gloried in the faith of Christ, and looked for his appearing to set up his kingdom on the earth and reign over a redeemed world, as the great King of nations. But the time was not yet. Has it never struck you in reading the epistles of St. Paul, that he is at so great pains to disabuse the minds of the Christian converts of the impression that Christ was *speedily* to come? Whilst continually holding forth the glorious truth, that their risen Lord would, in the fulness of time, be revealed in flaming fire to take vengeance on his foes, and to gather together in one fold the mighty multitude whom no man can number, and cheering the souls of God's people with that blessed hope, even the glorious appearing of the great God, our Saviour Jesus Christ, who shall change these vile bodies, and fashion them like unto his own glorious body, by that power wherewith he is able to subdue all things unto himself, the apostle is nevertheless plain and emphatic in the declaration, that before this great day of adoption, even the redemption of the body, for which all God's new creation groaned in earnest, longing expectation, the Spirit expressly declared, a great falling away should come, and the man of sin, the son of perdition must be revealed, whose coming is after the working of Satan, with all power, and signs, and lying wonders, and with all deceivableness of unrighteousness in them that perish. Thus he writes in his epistle to Timothy, describing the apostacy by infallible marks, and pointing to Rome, the mystic Babylon, as that

Wicked One, which shall be known, by its giving heed to seducing spirits and doctrines of dæmons, speaking lies in hypocrisy, forbidding to marry, and commanding to abstain from meats, and he declares to his Son in the Gospel, "If thou put the brethren in remembrance of these things, thou shalt be a good minister of Jesus Christ, nourished up in the words of faith and of good doctrine, whereunto thou hast attained." Let no man, therefore, tell us that we sin against charity, when we hold forth the testimony of sacred truth and warn every man to beware of that Wicked One, for we are fulfilling an express command of the Holy Ghost. So again, in his second epistle to the Thessalonians, St. Paul adjures the Church, "Now, we beseech you, brethren, by the coming of our Lord Jesus Christ, and by our gathering together, unto him, that ye be not soon shaken in mind, or be troubled, neither by spirit, nor by word, nor by letter as from us, as that the day of Christ is at hand. Let no man deceive you by any means; for that day shall not come, except there come a falling away first, and that Man of Sin be revealed, the son of perdition, who opposeth and exalteth himself above all that is called God, or that is worshipped; so that he, as God, sitteth in the temple of God, showing himself that he is God. Remember ye not, that when I was yet with you, I told you these things? And now ye know what withholdeth that he might be revealed in his time; for the mystery of iniquity doth already work; only he who now hindereth will hinder, until he be taken out of the way" (viz. the ancient Roman empire). "And then shall that Wicked One be revealed, whom the Lord shall consume with the spirit of his mouth, and shall destroy with the brightness of his coming; even him, whose coming is after the working of Satan, with all power, and signs, and lying wonders, and with all deceivableness of unrighteousness in them that perish, because they received not the love of the truth that they might be saved." Now, I ask, what church or what system of religion, calling itself Christian, answers the description of this inspired prophetic portrait, save the Church of Rome?

The Pope is styled, "our Lord God," "another God upon the earth." The priest of Rome is taught that in the confessional, he sits AS GOD; this is the literal language of the Romish dogma, and if questioned upon oath, respecting any thing that he has learned at that tribunal, he may deny all knowledge of it, because there, he knows nothing as a man, but all he there learns and knows, HE KNOWS AS GOD! Could there be a more perfect counterpart to the declaration of the prophetic apostle? And well does the entire history of that terrible apostacy answer the description of St. Paul! From the seventh century, in which Gregory assumed the title of Universal Bishop, or certainly from the eighth century, in which the claim to temporal and spiritual supremacy was combined in the Roman pontiff, that Wicked One has been the great agent and vice-regent of the Destroyer upon earth. When, by the wiles of the devil, men had been corrupted from the simplicity of the gospel, and human traditions and pagan idolatry had polluted the temples of the Most High, then the Man of Sin stood forth revealed, as the dragon and the beast, foretold by Daniel and John, and the mother of harlots and of the abominations of the earth began to quaff the blood of the saints and of the martyrs of Jesus, until in the madness of her intoxication, she had filled her temples with her names of blasphemy, and waged a war of extermination upon all who would not worship at her shrine. The coming of that apostacy is after the working of Satan the Destroyer! Papal Rome has shed the blood of millions upon millions of the human race! She has been for many centuries the motive power originating wars that have desolated Europe and the world. She has led on the cruel hosts who have waged a war of utter extirpation against the followers of Jesus. She has written her history for the last twelve hundred years in blood. There it is—blood, innocent blood, staining the hands and the face and the garments of the mighty murderer. And the record is not yet ended. Still she lives to deceive the nations, to stir up devastating wars, and to wear out the saints of God from every corner of her empire. Never yet has she set foot upon soil and conquered it for herself, that she has not baptized it with the blood of the saints of the Most High! Never, in one single instance, has she failed with marvellous consistency, to prove her hatred of the truth, and to record it in the blood of its confessors! But vast as the desolations are, accomplished by her instrumentality in the murder of them who held fast the word of truth, the aggregate of woe which she has entailed on the Church, gives but a faint idea of the conquests of the Destroyer. When she has prevailed against the people of God and blotted out their name from their earthly home, heaven has gained what a wicked world has lost. They are taken from scenes of suffering in which they have expired, to dwell with Jesus Christ in heaven; snatched from the power of Satan, and safe for ever from his wrath, they go to join the noble army of witnesses slain for the word of God, and to rejoice amid all the honors and crowns of conquerors. Not so, they who have not the seal of God in their foreheads—not so, they who bear upon their brow the mark of Antichrist. They fall under the power of the destroyer, and are ruined eternally. Look at the countless millions who have followed the cunning fables of the Man of Sin. Speak not of salvation for those who are the slaves of the strong delusion, by which they change the truth of God into a lie, and then believe it; for God says, they shall all be damned who have pleasure in unrighteousness. Tell us not we sin against charity, when we declare that the smoke of their torment shall ascend up for ever and for ever, who worship the beast and his image, for God himself declares, they shall have their portion in the burning lake for ever. Talk not of a reformation of the papacy, for the Lord proclaims that it shall be destroyed. The cry of innocent blood has ascended to heaven from the earth against that wicked one for twelve long centuries—innocent blood, which God would not forgive to Jerusalem, which he never will forgive to Rome! That day is hastening on—the day of God's judgment upon the great harlot, the precursor of the judgment of Apollyon when Satan shall be dragged down to the pit and be chained amid its darkness for a thousand years. Ere long the mighty challenge will be heard, sounding through all the spacious mansions of heaven, "Rejoice over her, thou heavens, and ye holy apostles and prophets, for God hath avenged you on her," and the universe of God will send back the shout of approval, and cry Amen! to the sentence of the righteous judge. All you who love the Saviour and pray for the triumph of his truth, will join with all redeemed and holy beings, on that day, and the shout will go up from heaven and earth, "Alleluia, salvation, and glory, and honor, and power unto the Lord our God, for true and righteous are his judgments; for he hath judged the great whore which did corrupt the earth with her fornication, and hath avenged the blood of his servants at her hand! Alleluia, the Lord God Omnipotent reigneth!"

Nor are these the only victims of the Destroyer. All, in every age, who have rejected the light of the sacred Scriptures—and have kindled a fire and compassed themselves with the sparks of their own kindling, and walked in the light of their fire, shall have this, at the hands of the great God, they shall lie down in sorrow. It is by the word of God's lips only, that men are kept from the paths of the destroyer. If they reject or pervert the truths essential to the soul's salvation they shall perish;

yea, if they profess to hold that truth, and have not the faith in Christ which makes the believer one with him, the Lord Jesus will not own them! Alas! for them who blaspheme his name, and change the truth into a lie! Alas! for them who pervert the right way of the Lord, blind their own eyes through prejudice and unbelief, fall into the ditch themselves and drag others down with them! Alas! for them, who rail against the Bible and the Sabbath, and the church, and the ministers of the living God! Wo—wo to them, when God shall deal with them! Yea, wo to them who love the world and the things of the world, and whose religion never carries them above conformity to the world! They are all—all slaves of Satan, and all, dying as they now live, shall be the victims of Apollyon for ever! Oh! believe it! Remember it! There is no safety in this world, or out of it, for you, for me, for all to whom God has given a living soul, save alone in Jesus Christ. There is no peace here, amid earth's scenes of most enchanting loveliness, amid all that can please the eye, or that can gratify the senses, there is no peace save that which the believer finds at the feet of a crucified, risen, interceding Saviour! Would that you all might feel it, that you all would own it, that you would honour the testimony of the Saviour that was dead and is alive—the Alpha and Omega, the First and the Last, who liveth for evermore! Shake off the sloth that benumbs you. Rouse from your lethargy! This cry of "peace, peace, when there is no peace," is the opiate of Apollyon. God lighten your eyes, lest you sleep the sleep of death! Arise, call upon your God! The Destroyer is in your path. Time is waning. The hours of salvation are fast flitting from you! Soon you will be in the spirit-world. Soon you will be, either saved or lost forever! To be impenitent and unregenerate is to be led captive by the devil at his will. You must come to the Saviour, if you would escape the Destroyer. There is no other alternative. If, when Jesus Christ shall consign Apollyon and his legions to that dark prison house, you would be saved from the doom which awaits the wicked, who will be accursed of God on that day, and depart into everlasting fire prepared for the devil and his angels—if you would join in the thanksgiving of them who bless God that the accuser of the brethren, who accuses them night and day before God, is cast down, then you must be prepared by grace to praise Him, who sprinkles from an evil conscience, and gives to them who are sanctified an inheritance among his saints for ever. Seek that grace now, give no sleep to your eyes until you have found it Never, never rest, until your feet are planted on the rock, from which you can look down upon the rage and malice of the Wicked One, and bless God for the shield of faith which quenches all the fiery darts of the Destroyer.

APPARITIONS.

Even a brief discussion of the topic to which these pages are devoted would be imperfect, without some direct allusion to the subject of apparitions. Can the departed spirit revisit the scenes in which it has been active during its abode in the body? And if this is possible, are these visitations matters of actual occurrence in our own day? These questions, though closely allied, are distinct inquiries. The former may be answered positively and without hesitation, but the latter is not so easily determined. That such apparitions are in the range of possibility, we might affirm on the simple ground that all things are possible which God, in his wisdom, sees fit to allow, but we have a still higher warrant, because the Scriptures plainly teach that they have actually occurred. The apparition of disembodied spirits is matter of record in the sacred history. The case of Samuel has already been noticed. The attempt to represent this as a juggling feat of the Witch of Endor only aggravates the difficulties of the narrative, and suggests inquiries far more intricate and perplexing than any which can invest the narrative if regarded as a plain statement of facts as they occurred. Besides, it would seem unreasonable to suppose, that the inspired writer would have failed to note the deception, and thus apprise the reader that there was no actual apparition, if such had actually been the case. One such instance is as decisive, as a hundred examples would be, in settling the question proposed in the former of these two inquiries. This, however, is not the only instance recorded in the Old Testament. The remarkable passage recorded in the Book of Job (ch. iv.) may be cited in the same category. "Now a thing was secretly brought to me, and mine ear received a little thereof. In thoughts from the visions of the night, when deep sleep falleth on men, fear came upon me, and trembling, which made all my bones to shake. Then a spirit passed before my face, the hair of my flesh stood up: It stood still, but I could not discern the form thereof: an image was before mine eyes; there was silence, and I heard a voice saying, Shall mortal man be more just than God? Shall a man be more pure than his Maker?" These are the only examples afforded in the Old Testament record. The New Testament presents an instance of this character in the narrative of our Saviour's transfiguration, when Moses and Elias appeared on Mount Tabor, and conversed with him. Incidentally also, the book of the New Covenant affords no little suggestive light on the subject. When our Lord walked on the waves of the Sea of Galilee, and the ship in which his disciples were, "was now in the midst of the sea, tossed with waves; for the wind was contrary; in the fourth watch of the night, Jesus went unto them, walking on the sea. And when the disciples saw him walking on the sea, they were troubled, saying, It is a spirit! and they cried out for fear!" The disciples of our Lord, evidently believed that the apparition of a departed spirit was possible, and neither on this occasion, nor subsequently after his resurrection, did he rebuke them for inclining to a superstitious credulity. He reassures them on the sea of Galilee and dissipates their terror by the words: "Be of good cheer; it is I; be not afraid." (Matt. xiv.) Again, after he was risen from the dead, when the eleven were together, wondering at the tidings of the Lord's resurrection, and of his actual appearance to some of his brethren, "As they thus spake, Jesus himself stood in the midst of them, and saith unto them, Peace be unto you. But they were terrified and affrighted, and supposed that they had seen a spirit. And he said unto them, Why are ye troubled? And why do thoughts arise in your hearts? Behold my hands and my feet that it is I myself: handle me and see; for a spirit hath not flesh and bones as ye see me have." (Luke xxiv.) No intimation is given in the Saviour's answer that the belief in the possibility of an apparition of "a spirit" was contrary to the faith of the gospel, but our Lord shows them, that in this instance, as in the former, they were mistaken, because in his bodily presence, he there stood before them. We cannot pass from the record of the Evangelists without a brief notice of other suggestive passages. Those words of the Saviour, (Matt. xii. 43,) bear at least suggestively on this topic—"When the unclean spirit has gone out of a man, he walketh through dry places, seeking rest, and findeth none," &c. We are told by some expositors that our Lord in this instance accommodates himself to the popular notions of the Jews, by way of amplifying an illustration! Surely this is a dangerous and most pernicious suggestion. If we are required to admit that HE could pander to the errors of popular superstition in one instance, why may he not have done so in a hundred cases, and in all that he said? Then our faith in the gospel must stand on a very insecure foundation. Jesus Christ never winked at error, never endorsed it, never taught it. His testimony in all its details was always truth and never falsehood, and the positive assertion that such is the truth respecting "the unclean spirit" is sufficient, whether the fact stands as an insulated portion of revealed truth, or whether it be employed as an illustration of another doctrine.

The parable of Dives and Lazarus, if parable it be, and not a narrative of actual fact, presents another suggestion relevant to this subject. Dives prays that Abraham may send Lazarus to his father's house, "For I have five brethren: that he may testify unto them, lest they also come into this place of torment. Abraham saith unto him, They have Moses and the Prophets; let them hear them. And he said, Nay, Father Abraham, but if one went unto them from the dead, they will repent. And he said unto him, If they hear not Moses and the prophets, neither will they be persuaded, though all rose from the dead." (Luke xvi.)

The relevancy of this quotation is not impaired by the objection that it occurs in the course of a parable, even admitting that it is a parable. The idea that our Lord would or could select the errors of "popular superstition" in order to illustrate the truths which he designed to inculcate is injurious, and should never for a moment be tolerated. The refusal of the request of Dives, by no means proves that the apparition of a departed spirit is not possible, or that it is never permitted, but it does establish the truth, that the word of the living God, is the instrumentality by which sinners are to be converted.

If we pass from the Evangelists to other portions of the New Testament, we find one additional instance, which stands in harmony with all that precede it. Peter was put in prison by order of Herod, after James, the brother of John, had been put to death. The angel of the Lord delivers him from his bonds. He goes "to the house of Mary, the mother of John, whose surname was Mark, where many were gathered together praying. And as Peter knocked at the door of the gate, a damsel came to hearken, named Rhoda. And, when she knew Peter's voice, she opened not the gate for gladness, but ran in, and told how Peter stood before the gate. And they said unto her, Thou art mad. But she constantly affirmed that it was even so. Then, said they, It is his angel," &c. (Acts xii.) There can be no doubt, in view of these citations, that the apostolic belief was clearly in favor not only of the possibility of such apparitions, for on that point, they could have no hesitation, but of the actual occurrence of these phenomena. The instances recorded in the Scriptures are conclusive in these two respects. If the sphere of inquiry be enlarged so as to include the visitations of angels and their actual apparition, the evidence furnished by the Scripture, becomes overwhelming, but the subjects are properly distinct, though nearly related to one another. The inquiry relates to the apparition of *departed* spirits, and yet it is not easy to understand, if it be admitted that angels have appeared to men, why departed spirits may not also have assumed a visible form. The former of the two questions which we have proposed, viz.: Is it possible that a *departed spirit should revisit the scenes in which it has been active during its abode in the body?* we are prepared to answer in the light of the Scriptures, thus—The thing is not impossible, for apparitions are spoken of in the oracles of God, as having actually occurred, and there are incidental suggestions which seem to take this truth for granted. This, we regard as a fair and candid conclusion. Now, if we are asked, *are such visitations matter of actual occurrence in our own day?* We must answer, we hold that such phenomena are still as much in the range of *possibility* as they ever have been, and we can find no word in the Scriptures which would lead us to infer that they are excluded from the experience of any age of the world; but it is equally plain from the whole inspired testimony that they are of rare occurrence. One instance, or at the most two examples are found in the whole of the Old Testament, and but a single instance of an actual though duplicate apparition is recorded in the New Testament. If they occur, therefore, they are exceptions to the rule. They may be permitted in the providence of

God for the accomplishment of some specific purpose, but in all probability, not one in a hundred of the phenomena of so called spectral or spiritual apparitions can bear the scrutiny of rigid investigation. Sound philosophy does not lead us to deny the possibility of a basis of truth being at the foundation even of a popular superstition. It is not easy to account for the prevailing notion of all ages and nations on this subject, if we regard it as wholly a figment of the imagination. We would rather discern in it, a great moral use, and suppose that it might be providentially allowed, in order to keep the important truth present to the mind, that there is an actual separate existence of the disembodied spirit, in opposition to the Sadduceeism of all ages. An eloquent writer makes the following judicious reflections, with which we conclude this chapter.*

"Thoughts of a deceased friend become sometimes, and in some mental constitutions, so vivid for a moment, that the difference between recollection and present reality is all but imperceptible. The departed spirit seems even present to the inward eye; his influence is actually and most powerfully felt; may he not be indeed near, though invisible?

* Rev. Dr. Burgess, Bishop of the Protestant Episcopal Church, in Maine. See his work, entitled, "The Last Enemy, Conquering and Conquered," pp. 177–179.

This is the question which prepares the mind for a belief in outward though dim and momentary apparitions. Of all this, the most remarkable instance on record may possibly be that of Emanuel Swedenborg, whose grotesque reveries appear to have been so habitually intense that he no longer distinguished between these and the firmest spiritual realities. But Wesley, also, who knew Swedenborg and believed him insane, has spoken of his own clear conviction, that the strong impression on his own mind of the images of deceased friends, at particular moments, was produced by their actual, invisible presence. Oberlin supposed that for many years he enjoyed intimate communications with the dead. It is certain, that, in our dreams, the appearance of a deceased person is sometimes marked by a peculiar vividness, which fixes itself on the recollection, and revives the profoundest feelings. Many have had, like me, a stream of consolation from the beaming, beatified countenance of a friend thus restored in the visions of the night. Johnson hoped for himself some communication with his deceased wife; and Boswell affirmed that he had himself, under a like sorrow, 'had certain experience of benignant communication by dreams.' The same thing is perhaps still more striking in the waking thoughts of some, under great excitement of the nervous system, but quite without derangement of the understanding. A lady whom grief for the loss of a beloved sister had brought to a highly hysterical state, which continued for several months, was at once and for ever relieved by seeing, as it seemed to her, the clear appearance of her sister, who bade her be comforted, and assured her of her own happiness. Another lady, who was afflicted with a kind of fit that deprived her of sensibility to things around, constantly saw in this state her deceased sister and child, but on her revival recollected nothing.

"From such remembrances and impressions, to the thoughts of visible apparitions, the transition is not difficult. One may often be mistaken for the other; and there is in human nature a strong desire to believe. Perhaps most of the more credible narratives may thus be explained; but the great question itself is not quite solved, when the belief in apparitions visible to the outward sight is rejected.

"That the appearance, visible as well as invisible, of the dead, is possible, the instances related in the Bible are decisive. That they have ever appeared to the outward eye, except in those instances, can scarcely be proved from history, to the satisfaction of the skeptical, or even of the indifferent. That, however, the strongest sense of their influence, as if they were present, has often been impressed upon the mind, in those states in which visible objects have least control, is confirmed by ten thousand testimonies. That at such times there is a real communion between the living and the dead, and a real presence of the dead with the living, is a natural conjecture, which cannot be wholly disproved."

SPIRIT MANIFESTATIONS.

As a pertinent expose of the mad vagaries of Spiritualism, we append a review of Dr. Robert Hare's book, entitled "Experimental Investigation of the Spirit Manifestations," from the columns of the New York Independent.

Experimental Investigation of the Spirit Manifestations—Demonstrating the Existence of Spirits, and their communion with mortals. Doctrine of the Spirit World respecting Heaven, Hell, Morality and God. Also the influence of Scripture on the Morals of Christians. By Robert Hare, M. D., Emeritus Professor of Chemistry in the University of Pennsylvania, Graduate of Yale College and Harvard University, Associate of the Smithsonian Institute, and member of various learned Societies. New York: Partridge & Brittan.

Dr. Robert Hare, Emeritus Professor, &c., &c., and member of various learned societies, is also one of that class of persons "who have said in their hearts, there is no God." From some hints at his anterior history in the book before us, we gather that for upwards of fifty years he has been a "professor" of the grossest materialism, only distinguished from sheer atheism by the childish belief in a heathenish deity of "enormous, though not unlimited power." He has believed neither in prayer, nor in Providence, nor in a future life; neither in angel nor spirit. He has been without hope "and without God in the world."

Dr. Hare is also a chemist of good repute in the scientific world, who has distinguished himself by important contributions to science,—contributions, which, we believe, have been generally the result of a high degree of mechanical skill and ingenuity, rather than of eminent powers of scientific investigation. We are not aware that his character for veracity and integrity has ever been called in question.

From these conditions the book before us is a not unnatural result. Dr. Hare commences the examination of the "spirit manifestations," in the full expectation of being able to account for them on known principles of physical science. So long as he had to deal with physical phenomena alone, his researches seem to have been conducted with skill, ingenuity and discretion. And the process by which he has shown the existence of intelligent movements inexplicable on the ground of known laws or of ordinary human agency, appears to us conclusive and convincing.

But the moment that he comes to something which cannot be tested by his balance, or his re-agents, or his electrometer, —the moment that the possibility of some supernatural agency is admitted to his mind,—all his philosophical caution disappears. His mind is adrift, on an unknown sea, without a single fixed and settled principle by which to guide his course. He stands, like a child at a fairy tale, all agape for new wonders. And the stuffing of weak absurdities which he submits to swallow, without chewing or choking, can be appreciated only by one who has read through his four hundred and sixty octavo pages.

This is sufficient to account for the book as a phenomenon. It remains to criticise it as a book.

In a literary point of view, it is beneath criticism. It abounds with blunders in grammar, and outrages on rhetoric. The bits of classical learning, which are paraded here and there, would amuse the youngest classes in a grammar school. Painful attempts at versification limp drearily down many of the pages; and once or twice the reader is regaled with the melancholy and servile giggle of a superannuated pun.

Dr. Hare's experiments to test the existence of *intelligent movement of tables, &c.*, independent of ordinary human agency, were so conducted that they must be satisfactory to every reader who admits the veracity of the witness.

As for the evidence which he offers of the *interference of supra-mundane spirits*, it is totally insufficient, even although we admit, as we freely may, that there is no strong anterior improbability of such interference, either from reason or history, and that the tendency of Scripture is rather to countenance a belief in it. Some curious statements are made on respectable authority, and some preposterous ghost-stories are told on no reliable authority at all. But we do not feel called upon either to explain the former or to disprove the latter, before pronouncing the argument to be inconclusive.

The professed *communications* from the spirit-world in this volume, are liable to the objection which has been brought so justly against all their predecessors, to wit, that they communicate nothing not already known, except things which cannot be verified. It is curious to see how exactly these "revelations" tell over again the previously conceived opinions of the person through whom, or to whom they are made. Those addressed to the Doctor himself, generally begin with some highly complimentary remarks on his acuteness of intellect and nobleness of character, and with the exception of some remarks on the economy of the spirit-world, consist chiefly of the stale infidelity which he had learned from Tom Paine in his boyhood The Doctor himself says, "I do not conceive that in my change of opinion, I have been involved in any change of principle." (§ 660.)

The most amusing thing in the whole volume is a specimen of this correspondence between the revelation and the imagination of the medium, in the communication on page 104. It is from the ghost of a young lady, through a lady medium, and undoubtedly presents *a young lady's ideal of heaven.* We have space only to allude to the description which it gives of the heavenly residence of H. K. White. This is in the fifth heaven, (which seems to be associated in the mind of the author with the Fifth Avenue,) and is a perfect love of a "cottage, embosomed in trees and flowers," about which the "grounds are tastefully laid out." "The clematis and honeysuckle entwine their tendrils around the trelliswork of the door." Within, it is adorned with "most exquisite" statues, and furnished with extraordinary "couches and divans," and *such be-yu-u-ti-ful carpets!* In addition to this there is the best society in the neighborhood, such as "the Wesleys, Byron, Burns, Moore, Shelley and Scott," of whom the *Spirit Maria* "speaks in particular, because she is personally acquainted with them, being attracted to them by a congeniality of feeling." Can anything more be wanting to perfect bliss?

Another objection which has been brought against previous revelations, is equally good against these in Dr. Hare's book; to wit, that they are ridiculously unworthy of the minds of their pretended authors when living. Of course we cannot judge of the *ante-mortem* accomplishments of the "spirit Maria;" or of the late benevolent Mr. Wm. Wiggins; and as for Dr. Hare's chief familiar, it must be allowed that the twaddle of his "honored father," bears a strong family likeness to the twaddle of his father's son. But we must decline to believe that the spirit of Washington should occupy itself chiefly in meditation on the talents and virtues of Prof. Robert Hare. Neither will a reader of his correspondence when on earth, think it altogether like the man, that, when Dr. Hare addresses him with a eulogy, in eight doggrel stanzas which would be rejected by a country newspaper, he should reply as follows:

"My Friend:—How my heart swells with grateful emotion, at hearing that beautiful effusion from your lips! Yes, my friend, I strove while on earth, &c. &c.

* * * * * * *

"Your noble father is a friend of mine, and I feel a love for you commensurate with his worth. * * * *

"My friend, I sympathize with you in your arduous undertaking; but let me assure you that your reward will be greater than the suffering you have endured. Yes, most nobly you have fought against error; and you will yet place the banner of freedom high upon the battlements of truth. Farewell noble scion of a noble man!

"Geo. Washington."

Dr. Hare seems himself to have some misgivings about the value of the communications. He claims, indeed, that the communication of his "spirit father" contains in a few pages "vastly more knowledge of our happy prospects in the future world, than all that can be found in the Scriptures;" but he adds that his "experience does not tend to establish that there is less folly or more wisdom in the inhabitants of the spirit world than in this." A few other paragraphs are equally significant:

"870. By their existence in the spheres, it seems to me that spirits improve as to their talents, not as to their reasoning powers. They have a superior knowledge to that which we possess of their own world, but not of our sciences, as far as I have had means of judging."

"872. To me it seems that their happiness is due in part to self-felicitation and seeing everything under a rosy hue. They often advert to the superior height on which they stand without showiug that they see more in consequence."

"873. So far as I can judge, in some branches of knowledge, the spirits will improve by discussion with mortals. They will be *cured of some of their 'sky-scraping.'* "

"876. Very soon after my father began to communicate with me, nearly fourteen months ago, he said, 'We know little more in religion than you.' "

Indeed, Dr. Hare sums up the chief additions which the spirits have made to our stock of useful knowledge, as follows:

"1753. The most wonderful and important of all the facts communicated to me by my spirit father and subsequently sanctioned by a convocation of spirits, were the following:

"1. That there is a special spirit sun, concentric with our sun, which illuminates the spirit-world, without perceptibly affecting our visual organs. 2. There is a peculiar vital gas which spirits breathe, although inscrutable to our senses or chemical tests, which we respire in our spiritual capacity."

If these are the most important facts of the new revelation, it certainly is not worth while to give much attention to those of minor consequence. As for the "special spirit sun" we evidently have no concern with it; and it is difficult to see what use we can make of the "spirit-gas" until Dr. Hare shall have succeeded in bottling some for domestic consumption.

There is one difficulty, a fatal one touching all the spiritual communications, to which Dr. Hare several times alludes, but seems never to succeed in suggesting an explanation. It is this. *The spirits will lie.* Mr. Amasa Holcomb, an apostle of this new gospel, writes to the still unconverted Dr. Hare, as follows:

"You mention cases where the answers were not correct. Thousand of such cases might be furnished. In the presence of some of the mediums, almost all the answers will be false."

And Dr. Hare elsewhere tells us that "low, ignorant, foolish spirits, personate the spirits of eminent authors."

In these circumstances there is no certainty whatever to the devotee of the ghosts that his familiars may not be lying to him at any time or at all times. The only test of the spirit's identity seems to be to ask him several times over whether this is *really* he and not somebody else, and whether he is *really and truly*, telling the truth this time, for certain; a simple test, but unsatisfactory to bigoted unbelievers.

A very large portion of this bulky volume is taken up with a miserable, shallow and stale attack upon the Christian church, the Christian religion, and the character of the Saviour. The discussion is as unnecessary in the book as it would be in this notice. We cannot go out of our way on this occasion to answer for the hundredth time the vulgar blasphemies, for the hundredth time repeated, of Thomas Paine and Abner Kneeland; nor to expose the shallow and silly pretences of philosophy with which this "member ef various learned societies" insults the intelligence of the community, and seeks to impose upon the ignorant and simple. It may be well for the public that he has been permitted by God to expose the weakness and malignity of his mind. The church will need no warning to discover these "spirits" to be spirits of anti-Christ.

There is one moral which this book impressively teaches. No one will fail to read it in the sketch which the author gives us of the form of his religious exercises. A pitiable picture indeed! This dotard infidel, who has gloried for threescore years and ten in the shame of his unbelief, given over to strong delusion that he should believe a lie, bowing his hoary hairs before a pasteboard wheel, as he sits "in his solitary third-story room, *invoking his sister as usual!*"

The case of Dr. Hare is not a solitary one. Of the "converts to spiritualism" whose previous belief is mentioned in this book almost all were infidels, and some of them, like Garrison and Robert Owen, of a most degraded class. The "medium," Hume, claims among the disciples of his doctrine "upward of twenty-five thousand infidels and atheists in America." (§ 1578.) The lesson to be learned from such facts is this:

THERE IS NO SECURITY AGAINST FANATICISM AND SUPERSTITION, EXCEPT A REASONABLE AND INTELLIGENT RELIGIOUS FAITH.

CHAPTER I.

GUARDIAN ANGELS.

Are they not all ministering spirits, sent forth to minister to them who shall be heirs of salvation?—HEBREW i. 14.

Ah me! how many perils do enfold
  The righteous man to make him daily fall,
Were not that heavenly grace doth him uphold,
  And stedfast Truth acquit him out of all.
Her love is firm, her care continual
So oft as he through his own foolish pride
Or weakness is to sinful bands made thrall.

THE Apostle Paul makes the affirmation of the text in reference to Holy Angels; for the words present an affirmation in the form of a question. He speaks of the angels of God in the words immediately preceding those which are quoted above. He is arguing the divinity of the Lord Jesus Christ, and proves that the attributes, works and prerogatives of the Saviour, are such as never are and never can be predicated of a mere creature, however exalted. "To which of the angels, said he, at any time, sit on my right hand, until I make thine enemies thy footstool? Are they not all ministering spirits, sent forth to minister to them which shall be heirs of salvation?" The word "angel" is used in the Scriptures to denote the wicked spirits who followed Satan in his apostacy, as well as the holy intelligencies who retained their original holiness. Thus we read of "the angel of the bottomless pit;" "Satan and his angels;" and the Apostle Paul in enumerating the enemies who seek to separate the believer from Christ, but whose efforts shall all be unavailing, declares, that "neither death nor life, nor *angels*, nor *principalities*, nor *powers*, nor things present, nor things to come, nor height, nor depth, nor any other creature, shall be able to separate us from the love of God in Christ Jesus." Holy angels would never either desire or endeavor to separate God's people from Jesus Christ, hence the terms "angels, principalities and powers," in this passage, must have reference to evil spirits, the emissaries of the destroyer. The word angel is used also, occasionally, to denote ministers of the Lord Jesus Christ, who are his ambassadors and representatives. Thus the Epistles to the Seven Churches of Asia, recited in the Book of Revelation, are addressed to the angel of the several churches. The literal meaning of the word is messenger, and in a peculiar and restricted sense, it is applied also to the Messiah, as the anointed messenger or angel of the covenant. Jesus Christ was manifested on various occasions to the patriarchs and prophets of the old covenant, as "the angel of Jehovah," or the angel of Jehovah's presence. It was he who appeared to Moses in the burning bush. It was He who appeared to Joshua, as the captain of the Lord's host, when the tribes of Israel were going up to the extermination of the wicked Canaanites. It is of Christ that the Prophet Zechariah speaks in his vision of "a man riding on a red horse, who stood among the myrtle trees, and behind him were red horses, speckled and white; then said I, O my Lord, what are these? * * * and he that stood among the myrtle trees answered and said, these are they whom the *Lord* hath sent to walk to and fro through the earth. And they answered, *the angel of the Lord* that stood among the myrtle trees, and said, we have walked to and fro through the earth, and behold, all the earth sitteth still, and is at rest." (Zech. i. 8–11.) This is a lively illustration of the zeal of the heavenly messengers, who go to and fro over the earth to execute the commands of the Lord Jesus. The words of the apostle, in which he speaks of angels as ministering spirits, sent forth to minister to them that shall be heirs of salvation, present the solicitude of these holy beings in behalf of the church of God, in an affecting point of view. There is one who goeth abroad over the earth, walking to and fro, and attended by a multitude of principalities and powers, whose errand is to deceive, subvert and destroy. "Your adversary, the devil, goeth about as a roaring lion, seeking whom he may devour;" but there are others, no less quick and powerful, who wait upon the sons of men, and their errand is peace and love. How solemn the thought, that while the world "sitteth still and is at rest," while men are careless and unconcerned, suspecting no danger and listless respecting eternity, two worlds are in perpetual strife, and angels of light and angels of darkness are all looking on with interest, all on the alert, the one to push forward the chariot of salvation and spread the progress of the truth; the other to impede the progress of Christian faith and holiness, to corrupt the way of men, and change the truth of God into a lie. If the earth sitteth still and is at rest, heaven and hell are up and doing.

It is strange, that notwithstanding the instinctive yearning of the human heart after some positive knowledge of the spirit world, toward which he is flying on the wings of time, and though the Scriptures are so full of information respecting its inhabitants and their employments, Christians are so generally in doubt and uncertainty, and know so little of the revealed truth, which God has ordained for their special comfort and encouragement. Perhaps one cause, if not the main source of this loss of positive enjoyment, is to be found in the abuse of the doctrine. Angels and dæmon spirits, or the spirits of the departed, have been worshipped, and their aid has been invoked as intercessors at the throne of grace, and thus insult has been offered to the only Mediator who intercedes before the throne, but let us not, therefore, discard a precious truth. Holy angels are not to be worshipped, but they are to be loved. We cannot commune with them, but they can and they do minister to us. One of the oldest poets of England has beautifully expressed this thought.

"And is there care in heaven? And is there love
In heavenly spirits to these creatures base,
That may compassion of their evils move?
There is:—else much more wretched were the case
Of man than beasts: but oh! the exceeding grace
Of Highest God that loves his creatures so,
And all his works with mercy doth embrace
That blessed angels he sends to and fro,
To serve to wicked man—to serve his wicked foe!

"How oft do they their silver bowers leave
To come to succour us, that succour want!
How oft do they with golden pinions cleave
The flitting skies, like flying pursuivant
Against foul fiends to aid us militant!
They for us fight, they watch and duly ward
And their bright squadrons round about us plant,
And all for love and nothing for reward!
Oh! why should heavenly God, to man have such regard!"

"Are they not all ministering spirits sent forth to minister to them that shall be heirs of salvation?" And is it not a sweet and comforting thought, that ere long we shall see these bright and holy beings, who have watched and guarded and strengthened us in many an hour of peril and temptation? That we shall be as the angels of God, in the resurrection, our Saviour himself has declared. Though the bodies of the saints shall be raised again from the dead, and made like the glorious body of him, who is the first fruits of them that slept and the first begotten from the dead yet our affections, our desires, and it may be, our employments, shall be like theirs, and though ever a distinct race, yet will there be a bright family likeness among all the "sons of God." The man after God's own heart cries out, as he looks forth into the glorious world beyond this earthly curtain, "Oh! that I had wings like a dove, then would I fly away and be at rest." How sweet to hold communion there, where the spirit never faints through manifold temptations, or flags through weariness, with the bright messengers of love, who have bent over us in kindest sympathy when we were afflicted, who have suggested holy thoughts and fortified us when we were tempted, and who, from the cradle to the dying pillow, have hovered over our pathway and have baffled the foul fiends that sought our ruin, and failing there, are ever waiting to harass and perplex the heirs of salvation. Does not this thought add another charm to the Christian's hope of heaven? Christ is the great attraction. Christ in us, is ever the hope of glory, but does not the apostle invest Mount Sion with the additional delight of angelic fellowship, and communion with the spirits of just men made perfect, in that noble and glowing burst of holy transport? "Ye are come to Mount Sion, and unto the city of the living God, the heavenly Jerusalem, and to an innumerable company of angels, to the general assembly and church of the first born, whose names are written in heaven, and to God, the judge of all, and the spirits of just men made perfect, and to Jesus the Mediator of the new covenant."

CHAPTER II.

THE MINISTRY OF ANGELS.

What man is he who boasts of fleshly might,
And vain assurance of mortality,
Which, all so soon as it doth come to fight
'Gainst spiritual foes, yields by and by,
Or from the field most cowardly doth fly!
Nor let the man ascribe it to his skill
That thorough grace hath gained victory:
If any strength we have, it is to ill,
But all the good is God's, both power and even will.

LET us survey the practical ministry of holy angels, as we find it illustrated in the examples furnished by the living testimony of sacred Scripture.

A poor woman, the bondwoman of Abraham, fled from the face of her mistress, and left her master's home, to wander in the wilderness. Weary, care-worn and oppressed with fatigue and grief, she was resting on her dreary pilgrimage by a fountain in the desert of Shur. She deemed herself a forsaken outcast; no eye of human friend was near to watch her tears of sorrow, or to share them with her, but as she bows her head and weeps, she hears a voice that calls in the stillness of the wilderness, "Hagar, whence comest thou, and whither wilt thou go?" She answers the angel of the Lord, "I flee from the face of my mistress Sarai." He counsels her, "Return unto thy mistress and submit thyself under her hands," and then he comforts her, with the promise that her posterity shall be great. It was Christ himself who spoke to Hagar, for we read, "She called the name of Jehovah that spake to her, Thou God seest me." Does the great Angel of the covenant watch the poor slave? Does Jehovah pity the bondwoman who is a fugitive? He does; he bids her be content with her lot, and put her trust in him who is the Lord and King of all, and it shall be well with her. (Gen. xvi.)

Years rolled on, Ishmael was born and grew up a wild and haughty youth. Sarai sees him mocking, and jealousy, which is ever cruel, prompts her again to harsh severity. She says to Abraham, "Cast out this bondwoman and her son, for the son of this bondwoman shall not be heir with my son, even with Isaac." And in the morning early, Abraham arose and took bread and a bottle of water, and gave it to Hagar, putting it upon her shoulder, and she went away with her child, and wandered in the wilderness of Beersheba. And the water was spent in the bottle, and she cast the child under one of the shrubs, and went and sat down, a good way off, as it were a bow-shot, for she said, Let me not see the child die, and she sat over against him and lifted up her voice and wept. Has she forgotten him who called her in the wilderness of Shur? If she has, he stil lremembers the poor bondwoman. "God heard the voice of the lad, and the angel of God called to Hagar out of heaven and said to her, What aileth thee, Hagar? Fear not, for God hath heard the voice of the lad, where he is. Go, lift up the lad, and hold him in thine hand, for I will make of him a great nation. And God opened her eyes, and she saw a well of water, and she went and filled the bottle with water and gave the lad drink." Again we see God's pity for the bondwoman. Christ himself is ready to relieve the wants of the outcast and save the mother and her perishing child from death. If the poor and desolate trust in him they shall never be forsaken.

Abraham sat in the door of his tent on the plain of Mamre, in the heat of the day, and as he lifted up his eyes, suddenly, he saw three men stand by him, and he ran to meet them from the tent door, and with the reverence of genuine courtesy, though he knew them not, he bowed before them and entreated them, "pass not away,let a little water, I pray you be fetched, and wash your feet and rest yourselves under the tree, and I will fetch a morsel of bread, and comfort ye your hearts; after that, ye shall pass on, for therefore are ye come to your servant. And they said, So do as thou hast said. And Abraham hastened into the tent unto Sarah and said, Make ready quickly three measures of fine meal, knead it, and make cakes upon the hearth. And Abraham ran into the herd, and fetched a calf tender and good, and gave it to a young man, and he hasted to dress it, and he took butter and milk and the calf which he had dressed and set it before them; and he stood by them under the tree, and they did eat." Noble, disinterested hospitality was here. There is no stint, no grudging of the best, which his basket and his store, his flocks and his larder can afford; no cautious, hesitating glance, which makes the mute lips ask, whilst they are silent, *Who and whence are you?* Enough, they are strangers; they may be weary, let them rest—they may be hungry, they shall have refreshment. And then, how cordial is the welcome. Abraham feels that he is the honored party, and therefore he acts as though he craved a favor. "My Lord, if I have found favor in thy sight, pass not away." This is characteristic of a generous heart; it transfers the debt of gratitude from the guest to him who entertains. These men, who were passing by his tent, like strangers on the earth, were citizens of another country—transient visitors in human form. One of them was the Mighty Angel of the Covenant, and the rest were angelic attendants; and their errand to Abraham was twofold. The Lord comes to tell him that in Isaac yet unborn, the nations shall be blessed; and then as they rise up and looked towards Sodom, and Abraham with constant courtesy attends them on their journey, the Lord reveals his purpose to his faithful servant, and Abraham recognizing his heavenly Master pleads with him in behalf of guilty Sodom and the cities of the plain which had made themselves abominable. The secret of the Lord is with them that fear him. In reference to this incident, the apostle admonishes Christians thus: "Be not forgetful to entertain strangers, for thereby some have entertained angels unawares." In the same connection, we find another affecting instance of angelic ministration to them that shall be heirs of salvation. Sodom and the cities of the plain were doomed, but the Lord will not destroy the righteous with the wicked. The Lord knoweth the righteous and delivers him in the day of evil. The tempest was gathering over the wretched captives of Satan's power—the elements of wrath were moving on, surcharged with the vengeance of Almighty God, and though the sun shone brightly in the heavens, and no storm-cloud was visible in the horizon, or in the face of the clear sky, the burning coals and arrows of death were already prepared; but ere the terrible day of the Lord bursts in a tempest of fire upon the wicked, angels are sent as messengers of mercy to warn Lot, whose righteous spirit had been vexed, and bid him escape for his life, with all his house. He runs with eager haste to his sons-in-law and cries, with all the earnestness of a father yearning over the salvation of his children, "Up, get you out of this place, for the Lord will destroy this city;" but he seemed to them as one that mocked. They laughed their father to scorn. Oh! remember, it is ever a token of perdition, when ungodly children treat pious parents with contempt. Lot is constrained to leave them, and with a heavy heart he goes back to his home. God will wait no longer; the angels hasten Lot: "Arise, take thy wife and thy two daughters, which are here, lest thou be consumed in the iniquity of this city." Still he hesitates—he would fain save his sons-in-law, and carry all his household with him to the place of safety. "And while he lingered," the messengers from God "laid hold upon his hand and upon the hand of his wife, and upon the hands of his two daughters, the Lord being merciful unto him, and they brought him forth, and set him without the city," and then they utter those words of earnest entreaty, which are the type of God's warning to sinners in the gospel, "Escape for thy life, look not behind thee: neither stay thou in all the plain: escape to the mountain, lest thou be consumed." In wrath God remembers mercy. He shows his regard for his people, not only by saving them in the day of calamity, but he honors them when they pray for others, and spares a remnant of the wicked for their sakes. When the terrible words of the angel fall upon the ear of Lot, he cries out with the vehemence and boldness of faith, "Oh! not so, my Lord! Behold now, thy servant hath found grace in thy sight, and thou hast magnified thy mercy which thou hast showed unto me in saving my life, and I cannot escape to the mountains, lest some evil take me and I die—behold now, this city is near to flee unto, and it is a little one. Oh! let me escape thither; is it not a little one? and my soul shall live." Because it was a little one, he would argue, its wickedness cannot be so great. And now, the true dignity and person of the angel whom Lot addresses become apparent; it is no other than the angel of the covenant who had appeared with angelic companions to Abraham, in the plains of Mamre, and who comes again with a chosen messenger, to execute the wrath of heaven. He hears the prayer of Lot; "See, I have accepted thee in this thing also, that I will not overthrow this city, for which thou hast spoken. Haste thee, escape thither, for I cannot do any thing till thou be come thither; therefore the name of the city was called Zoar," *a little one.*

CHAPTER III.

THE ANGELS IN THE WILDERNESS.

"As he thereon stood gazing, he might see
The blessed angels to and fro descend
From highest heaven, in gladsome company
And with great joy into that city wend,
As commonly as friend doth with his friend;
Whereat he wondered much and 'gan inquire
What stately building durst so high extend
Her lofty towers unto the starry sphere,
And what unknown nation there empeopled were."

THE sons of Isaac were grown up; Esau, the first born, was a wild man, who cared not for the birthright which might pertain to him as the elder son. He suffered Jacob to supplant him, and sold his birthright in a fit of peevish weakness for a mess of pottage. When the blessing of Isaac, securing the promise to Jacob, had already been imparted, Esau sought it, and with frantic regret, hung imploringly upon his father, and with a great and exceeding bitter cry, said to him, "Bless me, even me also, O my father!" Bitter as that cry was, his poignant regret was unavailing; Isaac's answer was,

"I have blessed him, yea, and he shall be blessed!" The birthright privilege of supremacy was lost, and Esau could not regain it, though his father blessed him, and in God's name, promised him the fatness of the earth and the dew of heaven for his dwelling, yet Esau, having profanely sold his birthright for a morsel of meat, found no place for repentance, though he sought it carefully and with tears. The conduct, both of Jacob and Rebecca, his mother, was not approved of God, for though the Lord had ordained the blessing for Jacob, he never sanctions deceit for the accomplishment of his purposes; "he that believeth shall not make haste," and the consequences entailed by the carnal devices of unbelief, are sure, in the course of God's righteous retribution, to bring forth fruits of sorrow. Esau hated Jacob; he appears to have threatened the life of his brother; he became reckless of parental authority, and grieved the pious hearts of his father and mother by marrying the daughters of Heth. Fearing that the fury of Esau might burst forth like Cain's wrath against Abel, Rebecca sent Jacob away secretly, and directed him to seek a home for a season with his uncle Laban. And now Jacob is made to feel that privation and sorrow must be the fruit of fraud, and that they who *will be* rich, fall into temptation and a snare, even though by the grace of God, they may be preserved from the many foolish and hurtful lusts which drown men in destruction and perdition. Jacob is led by a way that he knows not, but it was the way of repentance and of faith. He had obtained his father's blessing first by fraud, and now that he is about to leave his home, Isaac, with full consciousness that Jacob was chosen of God, lays his hand upon the head of his son, and prays, "God Almighty bless thee, and give thee the blessing of Abraham, to thee, and to thy seed with thee, that thou mayest inherit the land, where thou art a stranger, which God gave unto Abraham." Jacob goes forth, a pilgrim on the world's highway, a solitary wanderer in the wilderness; and as he journeys toward Haran, "he lighted upon a certain place, and tarried there all night, because the sun was set, and he took of the stones of that place and put them for his pillows, and lay down in that place to sleep. And he dreamed, and behold a ladder set up on the earth, and the top of it reached to heaven: and behold, the angels of God ascending and descending on it." Shall we permit this vision to be shorn of all its meaning by listening to the objection that the ministration of angels in this passage is altogether figurative? Our Saviour alludes to its significance, when he says, "Hereafter ye shall see heaven open, and the angels of God ascending and descending upon the Son of Man." It is through Christ, who opens the way from earth to heaven, that the ministry of holy angels is secured to his confiding people; were it not that the Son of Man has by his death and triumph over the grave, and his atoning sacrifice and prevailing intercession opened up that new and living way, the angels of God would not be flying to and from the earth on errands of divine love. It is with reference to the Messiah, that the Lord, who stood in Jacob's vision above the ladder, declared, "in thee and in thy seed shall all the families of the earth be blessed." Thus Jacob owned the presence and the voice of God, when awaking out of his sleep he said, "Surely the Lord is in this place, and I knew it not. How dreadful is this place! This is none other than the house of God, and this is the gate of heaven." The vision which Jacob beheld in the wilderness was a vision of realities. Whether we wake or sleep, holy angels guard the rising up and lying down of those who trust the God of Abraham, ministering to the heirs of salvation. There are those, who certainly place more reliance upon the significance of dreams than is warranted by sound Christian philosophy, but examples of supernatural dreams occur so frequently in the Sacred Scriptures, that we must beware lest we fall into the opposite extreme of error. Under the Jewish dispensation, they were an appointed means for the special revelation of the divine will. God came to Abimelech in a dream. The angel of God spake to Jacob in a dream. The dreams of Joseph were prophetic, and such also were the visions of Pharaoh, portending the seven years of famine, preceded by seven years of abundance. At Gibeon, in a dream, the Lord appeared to Solomon. The visions of Daniel, in which prophetic revelations were made to him, were sometimes given in the same manner, and many more incidental allusions to the force and import of dreams as suggestive means, might be cited from the Scriptures. Neither are these instances confined to the Scriptures of the Old Testament. The husband of Mary, the mother of Jesus, was warned of God, both before and after the birth of the Messiah, by the same instrumentality; the wise men who had come from the east to pay their homage to the infant Saviour, were warned of God in a dream of the designs of the wicked Herod, and departed into their own country by another way. The dream which troubled the wife of Pontius Pilate and induced her to admonish her husband to see to it that his hands were clear of innocent blood, may properly be ascribed to the same agency or cause. Indeed, it is expressly foretold by the prophet Joel, as characteristic of the Gospel era, and of the last times, "Your old men shall dream dreams and your young men shall see visions."

As I am naturally led by the case of Jacob's dream at Bethel, to speak on this subject, I may as well, in this connection, throw out the suggestion, that the commonly received theory by which these phenomena, which are not merely mental but properly spiritual, are accounted for, seems to me scarcely consonant with sound philosophy. The spirit is evidently active, and from its nature must always be active, even when the body is steeped in a state of somnolence. The spirit is always awake; it cannot sleep; and I am disposed to believe, that persons may frequently learn more of their true character by a careful analysis of their dreams than is generally supposed. So long as we are in the body, our waking impressions of external objects must be made upon the mind through the medium of the senses, and when they are steeped in the unconsciousness of profound slumber, the views, scenes and objects which are still present to the mind, must be produced by means of other instrumentalities; and though I care not now to argue the point, I deem it probable, if not absolutely demonstrable, that such impressions are produced by the agency of unembodied spirits, who compass us about, whether we wake or sleep, and I cannot but believe, that the vision of angels, going to heaven from earth, and descending from heaven to this lower world, and hovering around the pillow of the slumbering pilgrim, has a significant bearing on this very thought. Nor, is it improbable, that visions of terror would continually make night hideous and render the approach of slumber a source of constant apprehension, were it not, that kind angels guard the pillow of them who trust in God, "and so HE giveth his beloved sleep."

CHAPTER IV.

MAHANAIM.

Jacob went on his way, and the angels of God met him. And when Jacob saw them, he said, This is God's host; and he called the name of that place Mahanaim, or "Two Camps." —Genesis, xxxii. 1—2.

The earlier portions of the life of Jacob are not of a character to engage the affections of the reader. It is not easy to divest the mind of those feelings of dislike which his selfishness provokes. Even when we follow him in his exile from home, a pilgrim in the wilderness, our sympathies are not cordially with him, for it is impossible to forget that this banishment from his father's house was a righteous punishment, entailed by the providence of God as the just retribution for his injustice to his brother Esau. Neither can we be satisfied with the plea, that Esau was a reckless and profane man, who for one morsel of meat sold his birthright. This cannot justify Jacob's indirection in obtaining it. True, the fraud was suggested by his mother Rebekah, but its perpetration was nevertheless the act of Jacob. The birthright in the order of divine Providence was designed not for Esau, but for Jacob, and he was doubtless aware of this purpose, but this can never sanctify the means which Jacob adopted in order to secure it. It argues a want of faith in God. "He that believeth shall not make haste," but calmly wait, until by means of God's own appointment, the desired consummation may be reached. One fact, however, will strike the reader most forcibly. The feature in the sacred history which distinguishes the book of God from all other books is its stern impartiality. Where, in all the narratives which it contains, can a single instance be cited of an attempt to gloss over the infirmities of character or the transgressions of right in the conduct of the best of all God's saints? The failings of the heroes or favorites of a historian, or a biographer, are usually concealed, or extenuated in all human productions, but in the Bible, facts are given and motives when known, are portrayed without even the appearance of an attempt to exaggerate their excellence, when worthy, or to palliate the wrong when they are sinful. This is strong evidence of the truth of the record; it bears on its face the marks of a divine original, for it is so unlike the history which men present, when they would set forth the characters or the exploits of the founders or ancestors of their nation. Moses was a Jew; and the five books known by his name are devoted from the history of the flood onward, to a delineation of the events in the ancestral history of the Israelitish nation, but the historian never once forgets his position. He never pauses to offer a solitary comment. He never presumes to offer an opinion. He writes as the scribe of Jehovah—His pen moves only as God guides his hand. Now, this is a fact worthy of attention in its bearing upon the internal evidence of the Scriptures. They teach that man is fallen, depraved, corrupt. Universal experience confirms the doctrine. The history even of the children of faith establishes it. Thus, the historic portions of the record concur with the didactic parts in proving that salvation is of grace, and that but for the renewing of the Holy Spirit, no man could hope for salvation.

In the continuation of the narrative, we find the same trait of character, selfishness, standing out prominently in the transactions of Jacob with his uncle Laban. There was, in fact, sharp practice on both sides. Laban was, however, more deeply involved in these matters than Jacob. Jacob could say with truth to Rachel and Leah, "Lo, your father hath deceived me, and changed my wages ten times." And yet whilst Jacob's conduct was strictly within the literal terms of the bond, a little more regard to the interest of his employer, would have been more consonant with the beautiful trait of that charity "which seeketh not her own," and with that lovely generosity, which invests the character of Abraham with so much lustre, and which teaches all who are trained in the school of Christ, to look every man, "not on his own things only, but on the things of others also." We must remember, also, that the patriarchal age was not bathed in the glory of that bright example full of grace and truth, which shines forth in the person of Jesus Christ. Though Christ was in the patriarchal age, revealing himself as the Angel of Jehovah's presence, and the Angel of the covenant, he had not yet appeared as the Lamb of God, except in the promises by which he was even then, the Hope and Consolation of Israel. Some better thing remained for us—Christ is revealed as our life, and has left us an example that we should walk even as he walked. He has taught us by his own precepts and his own pure example, and by the inspired lessons of his holy apostles, that we are to imitate others and be followers of them, only in so far as they followed Christ. But with him, we are partakers of the life that is in him, and the life which we now live in the flesh, we live by the faith of the Son of God, who loved us and gave himself for us, that we who live, should not henceforth live unto ourselves, but unto him that died for us, and rose again.

After the lapse of more than twenty years, Jacob was warned of God to depart to the land of his kindred, and gathering together his family, and the flocks which had earned, he availed himself of the opportunity afforded by the absence of Laban, who had gone to shear his sheep, to take his departure, without giving his kinsman any notice of his purpose. "Jacob stole away unawares to Laban, the Syrian, in that he told him not that he fled. So he fled with all he had, and he rose up and passed over the river, and set his face towards the Mount Gilead, And it was told Laban, on the third day that Jacob was fled." Incensed by this unceremonious departure of his nephew, Laban gathers his people together and sets out in pursuit. After a seven days' journey, he overtakes the fugitives in the Mount of Gilead. Here the Lord appears, in a vision by night, and says to him, "Take heed that thou speak not to Jacob either good or bad." Laban's whole conduct towards Jacob and his daughters was mercenary and covetous. He disposed of them for gain, as though they had been slaves, and made no provision for them, giving no dowry though he had abundance of wealth. Rachel, unknown to Jacob, had taken with her, or "stolen," the images that were her father's. What these images, or "teraphim," were is not certainly known. In all probability, they were similar to the Roman household gods, which were used for purposes of divination, or foretelling future events, in the practice of superstitious rites. They seem to have been figures with a human form; or at least with a human head, and were of various sizes. Whatever Rachel's motive was, whether superstition, covetousness, or as it might have been, a desire to convince her father of the impotence and vanity of these idols, she had no right to take them. Laban overtakes Jacob. He remonstrates with him, but in a tone subdued by God's warning, which he acknowledges as a restraint. In his closing words, there is however, a somewhat tart sarcasm—"And now, though thou wouldest needs be gone, because thou sore longedst after thy father's house, yet, wherefore, hast thou stolen my gods?" Jacob answers the first part of his question with the calm and honest reply, "Because I was afraid: for I said, peradventure, thou wouldst take by force thy daughters from me." To the charge of dishonesty and theft, he says, indignantly, "With whomsoever thou findest thy gods, let him not live: before our brethren, discern thou what is thine with me, and take it to thee. For Jacob knew not that Rachel had stolen them." Laban, true to his own suspicious character, commences a search. Rachel imposes upon her father by an artifice and eludes the scrutiny in her tent, and he searched, but found not the images. Indignant at Laban's discourteous suspicion, Jacob administers a sharp and merited rebuke, and in a strain of eloquent vindication, convicts Laban of covetous injustice, and depicts the hardships to which, for twenty years, he had patiently submitted. Ch. xxxi. 36—42. Before this rebuke, Laban quailed. He felt its justice, and, on the spot, entered into a covenant with Jacob, confirmed mutually by an oath and after offering sacrifice upon the Mount, and thus ratifying the compact by a solemn appeal to God, both verbally and virtually, they ate bread in token of amity, and tarried all night in the Mount. "And early in the morning, Laban rose up and kissed his sons and his daughters, and blessed them: and Laban departed and returned unto his own place."

Jacob was now rich in worldly possessions. Before he left the land of Syria, the angel of God had spoken to him in the vision of the night, and calling him by name, had told him, "I have seen all that Laban doeth unto thee. I am the God of Bethel, where thou anointedest the pillar, and where thou vowedst a vow unto me; now arise, get thee out from this land and return unto the land of thy kindred." Jacob was thus admonished, that the means which he had adopted to promote his own interest would have been utterly unavailing, but for the divine blessing. "Say not in thine heart, my hand and the power of my might hath gotten me this wealth," was the admonition which Moses subsequently addressed to the people of Israel, and which God's people in all ages should remember. They are never to forget, "It is the Lord who hath given thee all this wealth." Oh! God's blessing maketh rich. The selfish covetousness of Laban cannot hinder Jacob's prosperity. Let him change his wages ten times, still God makes the blessing sure and turns the very devices of jealousy into so many means of promoting the welfare of his servant. God has not forgotten the covenant which Jacob had made with him, at Bethel. Those words, as they fell from the lips of the solitary pilgrim upon the silence of the wilderness, were written in the book of remembrance, and that solemn vow of the poor, friendless wanderer, was recorded in heaven. "If God will be with me, and will keep me in this way that I go, and will give me bread to eat and raiment to put on, so that I come again to my father's house in peace, then shall the Lord be my God. And this stone which I have set for a pillar, shall be God's house; and of all that thou shalt give me, I will surely give the tenth unto thee." Now, at the end of more than twenty years, the Lord appears to Jacob and says,

"I am the God of Bethel!" Jacob had prayed only for food and raiment, and for a safe and peaceful return to his father's house. The God of Bethel gives him riches more than his heart can wish. Oh! how foolish, as well as wicked it is to distrust or doubt the providence of God. Faith always brings God's blessing; and that blessing makes a man rich and adds no sorrow. The pilgrim passing over Jordan with his staff, and weary with his lonesome journey, is guarded by the angels of God. They keep him in all his ways, lest at any time he should dash his foot against a stone. Food and raiment God has given him in rich abundance. Now, he is on his way to his father's house. He desires to return thither in peace, and the God of Bethel has promised him this mercy also. True, Esau has not forgotten the supplanter. Jacob remembers well that bitter cry of his disappointed brother; its tones have rung in his ears in the solitude of the desert, and in the visions of the night, and often that plaintive voice has startled him with its wail of anguish, "Bless me, even me also, O my father." He is on his way to the home of his childhood, to the land of his kindred. If he left it with an anxious heart, his mind is not free from apprehension, now that he is returning. But the Lord is mindful of him. Of this precious truth, Jacob had a comforting assurance. We read, "Jacob went on his way, and the angels of God met him. And when Jacob saw them, he said, This is God's host, and he called the name of that place, Mahanaim," or "*two camps*." Both the occurrence and the name are full of profound significance. Jacob's heart was full of misgivings. The Lord in mercy comes to him and whispers, "I am the God of Bethel." Jacob relies upon the promise, and in faith journeys toward his father's house; and now, the angels of God meet him. Was not this another precious reminder of the scene at Bethel, when, all alone in the wilderness, he beheld the angels of God around him, ascending and descending upon that mystic ladder, and felt comforted with the sense of God's protection? Did he call the name of that place Mahanaim, *i. e. two camps*, to intimate, that the host of God had been his protectors, when wandering from his father's house, and were still engaged for his defence, now that he is returning to the land of his kindred? Or did he wish to indicate that the host of God encamped before him, as the vanguard, and behind him as his rereward? It matters not. The truth abides the same. "The angel of the Lord encampeth round about them that fear him and delivereth them." Some good men have sought to prove from the Scriptures that

God gives to each of his children a guardian angel; this is not half the truth. He gives many. He gives a host. Yea, he gives two camps for their defence. He protects the children of Jacob from Esau on the one hand and from Laban on the other. He maketh his angels ministering spirits, messengers of God, sent forth to minister to them that are heirs of salvation. These little children in helpless infancy he loves. The Saviour takes them in his arms and blesses them. From the high firmament of his power and the brightness of his glory, Jehovah Jesus owns them as objects of his loving care, and he says, "Their angels do *always* behold the face of my Father in heaven." Yes! they have always audience when their errand is concerned with the defence of the feeble and the helpless. Precious truth; full of comfort to the doubting Christian, pressed with perplexing fears. "The angels of God met him." Hold on thy way, child of God! Every resting place in thy journey is a Bethel. Every stage in thy pilgrimage is Mahanaim, for two camps are with thee! How sweet, in this view are those blessings which the Psalmist pours upon the people of God! How profoundly significant that benediction—"The name of the God of Jacob defend thee!" What is the name of the God of Jacob? It is the God of Bethel! The

God who covenants to give thee, pilgrim of faith, food and raiment, to be thy God, and to bring thee to thy Father's house in peace! Behold, the land of thy kindred—the heavenly Canaan. There are many mansions in thy Father's house. Jesus, the angel of the covenant, has prepared a place for thee. In all thy journeyings, having food and raiment, be content. If the Lord is thy God, he will provide for thee. In all thy perils and thy perplexities, the name of the God of Jacob defend thee! That was a precious interview to Jacob, when, on his way, the angels of God met him. What they said, we know not. Whether they spoke with audible voice, we know not. Enough, they met him, and with joyful faith, he exclaimed, "This is God's host!" The sorest peril of his life was before him. He prepares to meet it. "And Jacob sent messengers before him to Esau, his brother, unto the land of Seir, the country of Edom. And he commanded them, saying, thus shall ye say unto my lord Esau, Thy servant Jacob saith thus, I have sojourned with Laban and staid there until now; and I have oxen and asses, flocks and men servants and women servants; and I have sent to tell my lord, that I may find grace in thy sight." A soft answer turneth away wrath, but Esau's anger was not so easily appeased. He had not forgotten his wrongs. For more than twenty years he had nursed his wrath. Esau's was a vindictive spirit. The messengers brought back the tidings, "We came to thy brother Esau, and also he cometh to meet thee and four hundred men with him." Greatly afraid and distressed, Jacob adopts measures to insure the safety of at least one-half of his people. He divides them into two companies and the flocks, the herds and the camels into two bands, and said, "If Esau come to the one company and smite it, then the other company which is left shall escape!" Then he betakes him to his strong refuge. He appeals to God for protection. He pleads the promises. He confesses his own unworthiness. He gratefully acknowledges the mercies he has received. He prays for deliverance. He tells all his fears and all the dangers which threaten him, and casts himself and the burden which weighs upon his heart upon the arm of the God of Bethel. Beautiful in its simplicity and earnestness is Jacob's prayer, "O God of my father, Abraham, and God of my father, Isaac, the LORD which saidst unto me, Return unto thy country, and to thy kindred, and I will deal well with thee: I am not worthy of the least of all the mercies and of all the truth, which thou hast showed unto thy servant: for with my staff I passed over this Jordan, and now I am become two bands. Deliver me, I pray thee, from the hand of my brother, from the hand of Esau, for I fear him lest he will come and smite me, and the mother with the children. And thou saidst, I will surely do thee good, and make thy seed as the sand of the sea, which cannot be numbered for multitude." He renews his efforts to appease his brother. Faith and prayer are never intended to supersede the practical duties of a Christian profession. They rather render these the more imperative. God uses means to accomplish his purposes. Doubtless he suggested by his good Spirit the very measure which his servant adopted to secure the desired reconciliation with his brother. The management of the details shows wonderful address on the part of Jacob. "He took of that which came to his hand, a present for his brother Esau: two hundred she-goats, and twenty he-goats, two hundred ewes, and twenty rams, thirty milch camels with their colts, forty kine, and ten bulls, twenty she-asses, and ten foals. And he delivered them into the hand of his servants, every drove by themselves; and said unto his servants, Pass over before me, and put a space betwixt drove and drove. And he commanded the foremost, saying, When Esau, my brother meeteth thee, and asketh, saying, Whose art thou? and whither goest thou? and whose are these before thee? Then thou shalt say, They be thy servant Jacob's; it is a present sent unto my lord Esau: and, behold, also, he is behind us. And so commanded he the second, and the third, and all that followed the droves, saying, On this manner shall ye speak unto Esau, when ye find him. And say ye, moreover, Behold thy servant Jacob is behind us. For he said, I will appease him with the present that goeth before me, and afterward I will see his face; peradventure he will accept of me. So he sent the present over before him; and himself lodged that night in the company. And he rose up that night, and took his two wives, and his two women-servants, and his eleven sons, and passed over the ford Jabbok. And he took them, and sent them over the brook, and sent over that he had. And Jacob was left alone; and there wrestled a man with him until the breaking of the day."—(Genesis xxxii. 14–24.)

"And Jacob was left alone." What were his thoughts in that midnight hour, it is not difficult to imagine. His soul was full of anxiety. On the one hand was the promise of the God of Bethel, encouraging him to hope for the best and discard his fears. On the other was his sin—he had been a supplanter from his birth; he had cruelly wronged his brother—he knew it; and conscious guilt is the parent of fear and bondage. The guilty sinner is a coward before God and his fellow man. Jacob felt his guilt in that hour, as he had never felt it before. His past selfishness was a sore burden. God had a controversy with him. With all the fatherly kindness he had enjoyed, Jacob knew that there was a point still unsettled between him and the God of Bethel. Many years had passed since the fraud which had dispossessed his brother had been consummated. God had not forgotten it. His love to his children never leads him to forget their sins, till he has forgiven them; and ere that forgiveness can be gained, they must wrestle for it. They who would enter heaven by Christ the door, must agonize to enter there. It was night—Jacob had gone out—the brook was between him and his company—and while musing in that lonely hour, he is made conscious of the presence of one who has been watching him, and who stands in the way to oppose his progress. "There wrestled a man with him, until the breaking of the day." Probably, at the outset, Jacob knew him not, but he was made sensible of the character of his antagonist whilst engaged in the contest. "And when he saw that he prevailed not against him, he touched the hollow of his thigh, and the hollow of Jacob's thigh was out of joint, as he wrestled with him." Then, he understands who it is with whom he has to deal. He is wrestling with the angel of Jehovah's presence. He is agonizing with none other than the incarnate God. He is laying hold of the strength of the Lord's Anointed, that he may be at peace with him. "And he said, let me go, for the day breaketh." No—this can never be—to let go now is to lose all. Still, though halting and weary, he clings to his adversary—he cries out, "I will not let thee go, except thou bless me!" That is the cry of faith—importunate, fervent faith that will take no denial. This ends the conflict. "And he said unto him, What is thy name? And he said Jacob. And he said, thy name shall no more be called Jacob—(the supplanter) but Israel (the prince), for as a prince hast thou power with God, and hast prevailed. And Jacob asked him and said, Tell me, I pray thee, *thy* name? And he said, wherefore is it that thou dost ask after my name? And he blessed him there. And Jacob called the name of that place Peniel, for I have seen God face to face and my life is preserved. And as he passed over Penuel, the sun rose upon him, and he halted upon his thigh." Mysterious, awful conflict! Glorious triumph—man wrestling with his Maker—a poor sinner striving with Almighty justice, and more than a conqueror through the power of Almighty grace! Follow the history of Jacob from the hour of that day when the sun rose as he passed over Penuel, until the day when his sons gathered round his dying bed and wept as they listened to their father's blessing, and all trace of the supplanter is gone—his life is the life of a prince—the selfishness of Jacob has vanished and every action bears the mark of a generous, noble, loving Israel! This was the great crisis in his history. Henceforth, the character of the man of God stands forth in the clear and noble proportions of an heir of faith, consecrated to the service and the glory of his Redeemer. God prospers him. Esau is appeased. Instead of lifting his arm in anger, "Esau ran to meet him, and embraced him and fell on his neck and kissed him; and they wept." How much better that tears of repentance should mingle and fall together in drops of forgiveness on the ground, than that the earth should drink the blood of brethren, slain in the fury of cruel revenge.

He with whom Jacob wrestled at the ford of Jabbok is the same who gives the blessing to them only who will not let him go. "The kingdom of heaven suffereth violence and the violent take it by force." Hast thou an unforgiven sin resting upon thy soul, and galling thee with its yoke of bondage, behold at midnight, or when the sun has risen, that man whom God hath made a hiding place and a covert from the tempest, is nigh thee, watching the throbbings of thy guilty heart and pitying all thy grief. Wrestle with him—lay hold upon his strength and be at peace with him. Never let him go, until he bless thee, and whisper, "Thy sins are forgiven." If the darkness of midnight be around thee, and not a ray of peace can reach thy poor soul or pierce the gloom of guilt that covers thee with a horror of great darkness, and thou be left alone with God, rest not! wrestle! never let him go except he bless thee! The day will break, the sun will rise on Peniel, and thy soul shall be bathed in the light of heaven! As a prince thou shalt prevail. The child of faith has power with God. And though thy flesh fail, and thy sinew shrink, and thou go halting, leaning like Jacob on thy staff, to thy dying day, that staff is the staff of promise and it shall comfort thee and dying thou shalt sing, "The Lord is my shepherd, I shall not want." Yea, thou shalt go on thy way and fear no evil!

CHAPTER V.

THE ANGEL OF DELIVERANCE.

THE King of the Chaldeans had been slain and Darius the Mede reigned over the conquered kingdom. He appointed one hundred and twenty princes, over whom he set three presidents; of these Daniel was first. The exaltation of this Hebrew aroused the jealousy of his associates, and and though he was exemplary in all his life, without reproach and full of wisdom, a sound statesman and a holy man, yea, for these very reasons, they conspired against him. "An excellent spirit was in him and the king thought to set him over the whole realm." His enemies watched him; they were spies upon his administration, but they could find no fault, nor occasion, for he was faithful; so that they came at last to the conclusion, that no occasion of procedure against him could be found, unless it were, "concerning the law of his god." They devised a plan, and it was proposed to the king, that by statute law, a decree should be issued, that whosoever should ask a petition of any, God or man, for thirty days, except of King Darius, should be cast into the den of lions. The king was flattered by the suggestion, and the statute was enacted. Daniel knew it, but, as he had always been wont, so he continued as heretofore, with his windows open towards Jerusalem, he kneeled three times a day and prayed and gave thanks before his God. His enemies reported this conduct to the king. Darius was sore displeased *with himself*, not with Daniel, but with himself, and set his heart on Daniel to deliver him, and he laboured till the going down of the sun to deliver him, but the enemies of the pious Jew persisted, "No decree, nor statute which the king establisheth may be changed," and the sentence was enforced; but Darius said to Daniel, "Thy God whom thou servest, he will deliver thee." That night King Darius spent in fasting, "Neither were instruments of music brought before him; and his sleep went from him. Then the king arose very early in the morning, and went in haste to the den of lions, * * and he cried with a lamentable voice—O Daniel, servant of the living God, is thy God whom thou servest continually, able to deliver thee from the lions?" And the answer comes back full of holy faith and peace, "O king, live for ever, my God hath sent his angel, and hath shut the lions' mouths, that they have not hurt me, forasmuch as before him innocency was found in me; and also before thee, O king, have I done no hurt."

Thus, in times of peril, "the angel of the Lord, encampeth round about them that fear him, and delivereth them." And as Daniel was defended and came forth unhurt from the den of lions, through the preserving power of a ministering angel, so are God's people, amid all the trials and temptations and dangers of life, protected, until the number of their mouths is spent, and they depart to dwell with Christ and holy angels and the spirits of the just made perfect, for ever. What heavenly sympathy follows the earthly pilgrim, though not a word is whispered audibly into his ear! How these holy angels bend with purest love over the wounded spirit, and seek to soothe the pangs of mental anguish! How they crowd around the faithful servant of God and strengthen the soldier of Jesus Christ, that he may cheerfully and joyously encounter hardness! No child of God is so poor, or so much an outcast, that holy angels do not pity him; his very poverty and desolation add fervour to their holy sympathy. Excellent in strength, shining with the peerless splendour of sinless and immortal beauty, these heavenly principalities deem it an honour to wait upon the lowly in heart, and to minister to the weakest of the heirs of salvation. They have ever gazed upon this world of ours as upon a province of God's empire, invested with peculiar interest. When the foundations of the hills were laid and the earth came forth fresh and glorious from the hand of the Great Creator, all these sons of God sang together and shouted for joy! When man fell and redemption was proclaimed, they wondered, and the mysteries which rebellious, unbelieving men despise and scorn, they desire to look into. They were the companions of patriarchs and prophets of old. They waited, looking for and hasting to the day when Shiloh should come; and when the infant Saviour was born and cradled in the manger of Bethlehem, heaven could no more contain its joy. Down from those glorious thrones—away from their wide dominions, the principalities of heaven came, flocking in a mighty host, and the glory of the Lord shone around them, making night brighter than the cloudless noon, upon the plains of Bethlehem, and the poor shepherds heard the first tidings of Messiah's birth from angels' lips, "Fear not; behold we bring good tidings of great joy to you and to all people; for unto you is born this day in the city of David a Saviour, which is Christ the Lord." Then that mighty chorus, unheard by men since the fall in Eden, rang through the arches of heaven, and sounded abroad over the wilderness of

Judea, "Glory to God in the highest, on earth peace; good will to men;" and ever since salvation has been preached through the blood of a crucified Saviour, and sinners have been brought to Christ, wherever and whenever the Gospel has triumphed, there has been joy in heaven among the angels who surround our heavenly Father's throne. "Are they not all ministering spirits, sent forth to minister to them that shall be heirs of salvation?"

CHAPTER VI.

THE HEAVENLY HIERARCHY.

Are ye for ever to your skies departed!
  Oh! will ye visit this dim world no more?
Ye whose bright wings—solemn splendor darted
  Through Eden's fresh and flowery shades of yore?

THE sympathy of holy angels in behalf of those who are heirs of salvation, is illustrated by numerous affecting incidents in the narratives recorded in the sacred Scriptures, a few of which have been already adduced. A careful analysis of the various passages, both in the Old and New Testament writings, which relate to angelic agency, will lead us to infer that the administration of the divine government is carried on through the instrumentality of spiritual agents, acting in subordination to the laws of Him, who is over all, God blessed for evermore. That various departments of duty are assigned to them, may be safely gathered from the variety of their titles. They are not all equal in wisdom, authority, or power. One star differeth from another star in glory. The analogy of heaven and earth, in this respect is the same. It is so now among the living on earth, and it shall be so in the resurrection. Men differ in their capacities, in their position, in their physical powers, and in the various circumstances and relations, which are designed to make them mutually indispensable to each other, so that all may contribute to the general advantage and welfare of Christian Society; and so in heaven, there are dominions and thrones; principalities and powers; cherubim and seraphim; there are angels who *excel* in strength. "He maketh his angels spirits; *His* ministers a flaming fire;" but all are ordained for the furtherance of the divine glory, in the sphere assigned by his providence; all delight to do his will, and are ever ready to fly at his command, for the execution of purposes of judgment and mercy. The *nature* of angels is sufficiently explained in the declaration of the Psalmist, "He maketh his angels spirits." Some have supposed, from a misapprehension of a passage in Genesis, that they are gross corporeal beings; "The sons of God saw the daughters of men that they were fair, and they took them wives of all which they chose;" but by the "Sons of God," in this instance, we are not to understand the angels, but the children of pious Seth, in opposition to the descendants of Cain. They were called "Sons of God" under the old covenant, because they walked by faith in obedience, just as under the New Testament, the Apostle John says, "Beloved, now are the Sons of God." This unscriptural idea respecting the nature of angels, was maintained by some of the most eminent of the earliest fathers of the Church, amongst whom were Clement of Alexandria, Origen, Cæsarius, and Tertullian; but their opinion was opposed on the other hand by Athanasius, Basil, Cyril, Chrysostom, and others. As for the value of patristic testimony on doctrinal subjects, few persons who have been at the pains to study their writings can come to any other conclusion, than that a large mass of worthless speculation is mixed up with unquestioned truth, and that as a general thing, very few among them had unclouded views of doctrines, which since their day have been established with a clearness and precision that have commended them to all evangelical Christians. The theory respecting the angels is a case in point. That angelic beings have, at times, assumed bodies and appeared in human form, is undeniable. It is plainly asserted in the Scriptures. The visit of angels to Abraham in the plains of Mamre, and the messengers who were sent to warn Lot to make his escape from Sodom, are alone sufficient examples of this truth. Their proper nature, however, is spiritual.

This excludes the idea of a gross, material form, but it does not therefore follow, that they are shadowy beings. The apostle declares, "All flesh is not the same flesh; but there is one kind of flesh of men, another flesh of beasts, and another of fishes, and another of birds;" and then he adds these remarkable words: "There are also CELESTIAL BODIES, and there are bodies terrestrial, but the glory of the celestial is one, and the glory of the terrestrial is another." He also makes the distinction between the natural body which is sown in the grave, and the *spiritual body*, which will come forth in the resurrection. Angelic beings may have bodies peculiar to their nature, and similar in some respects to the resurrection bodies of the saints, and though we are not concerned to broach or establish any novel doctrine, we would venture in passing, to suggest, that it may have been with reference to this, and to intimate that even angels may taste the sweetness of food, that the Psalmist says, alluding to the manna which supplied the Israelites in the desert, "Man did eat angels' food." It is hard for us, conversant as we are ordinarily, only with the grosser forms of matter, to frame any clear or satisfactory idea of a spiritual body, and yet enough is revealed in the Scriptures to establish not only its existence, but the wonderful powers and faculties with which it is and shall be endowed. The resurrection body of Christ was unspeakably glorious; it possessed attributes which belong not to the human body, in its present organization. Material objects were no impediment to its transition from one place to another. When the doors were locked, the Saviour appeared amidst his disciples, greeting them with the gracious salutation, "Peace be with you," and then again he vanished as suddenly out of their sight. In order to convince them that they were not looking upon a mere spectre, he tells them, "A spirit hath not flesh and bones as ye see me have;" and he bids them handle him, and thus convince themselves, by the demonstration of sight and touch, that he was indeed their risen Master. He showed the unbelieving Thomas not only the prints of the nails in his hands and feet, but bade him thrust his finger into the side wounded by the spear, and silencing every doubt as to his identity, constrains Thomas to exclaim in the fulness of overpowering persuasion, "My Lord and my God." Now, though we do not affirm that angels are furnished with just such bodies as the resurrection body of Christ, yet we may infer from the declaration of the apostle respecting CELESTIAL BODIES and bodies terrestrial, that analogous diversities exist in the spiritual bodies of the inhabitants of heaven and the terrestrial bodies which are peculiar to the earth; and what the Bible makes known respecting the body of Jesus, after the resurrection, may properly be adduced as additional evidence, guiding us to a knowledge of the truth, which at best, in our present state, must be only a faint apprehension. Hereafter we shall know, even as we are known.

CHAPTER VII.

THE INNUMERABLE THRONG.

The chariots of God are twenty thousand, even thousands of angels.—PSALM lxviii. 17.

THE Scriptures represent the number of holy angels as inconceivably great. Thus when Daniel describes the Ancient of Days, he says, "A fiery stream issued and came forth from before him; thousand thousands ministered unto him, and ten thousand times ten thousand stood before him;" and again the Psalmist declares, "The chariots of God are twenty thousand, even thousands of angels." The Apostle Paul, in his description of the heavenly Zion, speaks of "an innumerable company of angels," who constitute part of the general assembly and church of the first born, whose names are written in heaven. The Redeemer, in that hour of deepest humiliation, ere he hung upon the cross, when he was betrayed into the hands of sinners, and the impetuous Peter had drawn the sword in his Master's defence, said to him, "Thinkest thou that I cannot now pray to my Father, and he shall presently give me more than twelve legions of angels?" All these expressions are designed to teach that the number of the holy angels is exceedingly great. The testimony of the Scriptures respecting the employment of angels in the administration of affairs on earth is explicit. Though they are spiritual beings, they have power over material objects. The first mention of the cherubim in Scripture, is in connection with their commission to guard the Tree of Life with a flaming sword. In the description of the resurrection by St. Matthew, this truth is again taught with the utmost plainness. "And behold, there was a great earthquake, for the angel of the Lord descended from heaven, and came and rolled back the stone from the door and sat upon it." On the great day, our Saviour tells us, angels will be sent forth "to sever the wicked from among the just." The watchful care of angels as the guardians of God's people is taught by the Psalmist in the words, "He shall give his angels charge concerning thee, to keep thee in all thy ways, lest at any time thou dash thy foot against a stone." God keeps our feet from falling, but it is through the instrumentality of blessed angels. They act not on their own authority, but are sent forth as his ministers of mercy. The doctrine of guardian angels, like every other truth taught in the sacred Scriptures, has been abused and perverted. Angels have been invoked and worshipped, and thus honour has been paid to them which pertains alone to God. This is contrary not only to the first commandment, which prescribes, "Thou shalt have no other gods before me," or *besides me*, but it is forbidden by plain example in the holy writ. Thus, when overwhelmed by the preciousness of the revelation of heavenly things promised by the angel of God, who had been commissioned to show them to the beloved disciple, for the comfort of the church, and awed by the majesty and glory of the heavenly messenger, the Apostle John prostrated himself in adoration, he was rebuked. "And I, John, saw these things and heard them, and when I had heard and seen, I fell down to worship before the feet of the angel which showed me these thinge. Then said he unto me, 'See thou do it not: for I am thy fellow-servant, and of thy brethren, the prophets, and of them which keep the sayings of this book. Worship God.'" We find traces of a disposition to pay undue honour to angels in the apostolic age, hence St. Paul warns the Colossians, not only against the practice itself, but also against the argument by which it was then and is even now defended. On the plea, that greater humility is evinced, by invoking the aid of secondary intercessors, who are requested by their worshippers to secure the advocacy of Christ, the devotees of a corrupt and false Christianity, attempt to justify their idolatry, but the apostle utterly condemns both the theory and practice, which are alike of pagan origin. They are relics of the idolatrous theology of ancient Greece and Rome. Hence, he says, "Let no man beguile you of your reward, in a voluntary humility and worshipping of angels, intruding into those things which he hath not seen, vainly puffed up by his fleshly mind, and not holding the Head, from which all the body by joints and bands having nourishment ministered, and knit together, increaseth with the increase of God." Let us not, however, fall into error on the other extreme, through fear of offending through the sinful and false humility, proscribed by the apostle. Holy angels surround the path of the just, to aid, to comfort, to strengthen, and defend. We may not worship them, we may not ask them to help us, but we may think of them and love them. In close union with this thought, another is suggested, which may be properly noticed as a cognate subject; I mean the relation which we who are the living on the earth, sustain to the spirits of the departed. To pray for the departed, or to pray to them, are both absurd. Our prayers cannot help them, neither can the spirits even of the just afford us aid. If we are reminded that Dives, when in Hades, being in torment, lifted up his eyes and groaned out his sad complaint to Abraham, beseeching him to send Lazarus, that he might dip the tip of his finger in water and cool his tongue, we need only refer the objector to the Saviour's own narrative to prove that even in the spirit world, there is no communion or fellowship, between the spirits of the just made perfect, and the spirits of the lost: "Between us and you, there is a great gulf fixed: so that they which would pass from hence to you, cannot; neither can they pass to us, that would come from thence." How much less then, can we, who are still in the body, commune with them, who absent from the body, are present with the Lord? Neither do the departed saints go from their heavenly home in Paradise, to warn the wicked of impending wrath; for when Dives implores Abraham to send Lazarus, that he may testify to the five brethren who were in the rich man's father's house, and thus save them from coming to that place of torment, Abraham says, "They have Moses and the prophets; let them hear them. And he said, Nay, Father Abraham; but if one went from the dead, they will repent. And he said unto him, if they hear not Moses and the prophets, neither will they be persuaded, though one rose from the dead." They who are driven away in their wickedness, from the hour of their departure are in torment, typified by the symbol of flame, to denote the terrible torture of a wounded spirit. *They* dwell with Satan, the prince of the power of the air, and his fallen angels. They are the dæmon spirits spoken of in the Scriptures, and these may have communion with the wicked upon earth, but others cannot, except by the special permission of God, as in the case of Samuel. "Blessed are the dead that die in the Lord from hence forth. Yea, saith the Spirit; for they rest from their labours, and their works do follow them." Are we then to banish from our memories, the friends who have left us and gone into a better country? No. This is not the fruit of faith, or the evidence of fortitude. We are not to treat them as though they had ceased to have any existence, but we are to love them and think of them as loving us. We may commemorate the day of their departure. Will any Christian say, that the widow in her loneliness may not regard the anniversary of her pious husband's entrance into rest? Surely, we may send out our affections and desires into that heavenly land, and long to be, in God's own time, with them who have escaped from the wilderness, and are safe in Canaan. We may think of them as yearning over us with kindest sympathy and loving us with heavenly purity, for the God of Abraham and of Abraham's children, is the God, not of the dead, but of the living. They are with Christ, and as all the happiness and joy of heaven are summed up in that one expression, we may, ever with holy submission to the will of God, learn with the blessed apostle to say, "I desire to depart and to be with Christ, which is far better. It is right, therefore, to combine in our thoughts the holy angels, and the spirits of the just, for if we love Christ, and are faithful unto death, these will be our glorious companions for ever. Of all who love him, Jesus says, "Neither can they die any more; for they are equal unto the angels, and are the children of God, being the children of the resurrection." (Luke xx. 36.) The ministry of holy angels, as the defenders of God's own people, is illustrated by a variety of incidents in the sacred Scriptures. Under the old covenant, it was a source of consolation in times of peril and anxiety. Thus, when Abraham was old and well stricken in age, he sent his eldest servant, having first required an oath from him, that he would not take a wife for Isaac of the daughters of the Canaanites, and bade him go to the patriarch's own country and kindred, and choose a wife for Isaac. The journey was long and arduous, and the errand was one deeply affecting the peace and happiness of Abraham in his old age, but the faith of Abraham was not to be daunted by the dangers which beset the enterprise, and with holy confidence in God and in the guardian care of ministering angels, the messengers of God; he says "The Lord God of heaven, which took me from my father's house and from the land of my kindred, and who spake unto me and sware unto me, saying, Unto thy seed will I give this land: he shall send his angel before thee, and thou shalt take a wife unto my son from thence." God did not put the confidence of his servant to shame; he sent his angel before his face to prosper Eleazar on his pious errand, and brought Rebekah to his master's house, by the special guidance and appointment of the Lord.

CHAPTER VIII.

ANGELIC PROTECTION.

He shall give his angels charge over thee, to keep thee in all thy ways.

WHEN Moses stood on the borders of Edom with the people of Israel, he sent messengers from Kadesh to the king of that country, saying "Thus saith thy brother Israel, Thou knowest all the travail that hath befallen us; how our fathers went down into Egypt, and we have dwelt in Egypt a long time; and the Egyptians vexed us and our fathers, and when we cried unto the Lord, he heard our voice and sent an angel, and hath brought us forth out of Egypt, and behold we are in Kadesh, a city in the uttermost of thy border; let us pass I pray thee through thy country, * * * *but* Edom refused to give Israel passage." Here is an allusion to the same guardian office of the holy angels, who like the bright lightnings answer the call of Jehovah, saying, "Here are we," and though the promise was not yet recorded in the book of the law, yet he gave his angels charge concerning Israel, "to keep him in all his ways." The words appear originally to have been spoken respecting the Messiah, and Satan applies them to the Saviour in his temptation, when urging the Redeemer presumptuously to cast himself from the pinnacle of the temple, garbling the text, however, by omitting the qualification, "in all thy ways." We have no promise of angelic protection, if we presumptuously rush into danger, but so long as we are in the King's highway, his heavenly legions plant their bright squadrons round about us to deliver and defend the pilgrims to the heavenly country. The declaration of the Psalmist was especially verified in the personal history of Christ. The angel of the Lord appeared to Joseph and bade him take the young child and his mother and flee into Egypt, adding, "be thou there, until I bring thee word, for Herod will seek the young child to destroy him." When Jesus was weary and exhausted with fasting, after his temptation, "behold angels came and ministered unto him." In Gethsemane, when the Redeemer was prostrate on the cold earth, and his sweat, wrung from him in his agony was as it were great drops of blood, falling down to the ground, "there appeared an angel unto him, from heaven, strengthening him." Angels came to share in the joy of the resurrection morning, they rolled the great stone from the mouth of the sepulchre. They entered the tomb where Jesus had lain, and filled the dark grave with the glory of heaven. They were the first to announce to the wondering disciples, as they gazed upon the place where Jesus had slept, "he is not here, he is risen." They attended him, at his triumphant ascension from Bethany, and shouted, as their ascending King, making the cloud his chariot, was taken out of the sight of his disciples, "Lift up your heads, O ye gates; and be ye lifted up, ye everlasting doors, and the King of glory shall come in. Who is this King of glory? Jehovah strong and mighty. Jehovah strong in battle. Lift up your heads, O ye gates; even lift them up, ye everlasting doors; and the King of glory shall come in. Who is this King of glory? Jehovah of hosts; he is the King of glory!" And whilst heaven's eternal dome rang with the applauding shouts of the principalities and powers of glory, and the thrones and dominions of celestial might came forth with all their hosts, to adore their King and bid him welcome to the mediatorial majesty, purchased by his death and resurrection, behold the sympathy of heaven shines forth in behalf of the sorrowing disciples, who with tearful eyes watch the retiring form of their ascending Master, until he is visible no longer, and "two men stood by them in white apparel, which also said, Ye men of Galilee, why stand ye gazing up into heaven? This same Jesus which is taken up from you into heaven, shall so come in like manner as ye have seen him go into heaven." Thus, in all his ways, from his advent to his ascension; from the manger-cradle in Bethlehem to the cross on Calvary; and from the sepulchre in Joseph's garden to Mount Olivet, whence Jesus ascended to the throne of mediatorial glory, angels attended the Redeemer as their Prince, wondering at the depths of his condescending love, and sharing in the triumphs of his grace. And when the apostles went forth to proclaim the glad tidings of great joy, the angels of God still waited on them to keep them in all their ways. With mighty signs and wonders, the truths of the Gospel were attested by the Holy Ghost. Diseases fled, dæmons were cast out, the very dead were raised, at the word of the ordained missionaries of the Saviour. Moved with indignation and envy, the Sadducees and the high priest of Jerusalem, beholding the success of the Gospel, laid violent hands on Peter and the apostles and cast them into prison, "but the angel of the Lord by night opened the prison doors and brought them forth and said, Go, stand and speak in the temple, all the words of this life;" and the next morning early, they were found again proclaiming Jesus and the resurrection as the hope and refuge of dying sinners, and fearlessly declaring that they must obey God rather than men. A time of persecution came. Herod killed James, the brother of John, with the sword, and seeing that this pleased the Jews, he proceeded to take Peter also, but prayer was made for him without ceasing by the brethren, and while the apostle was sleeping calmly between two soldiers, bound with two chains, and the keepers were standing before the prison-gate, the angel of the Lord came upon him and light shone in the prison, and he "smote Peter on the side, and raised him up, saying, Arise up quickly; and his chains fell off from his hands. And the angel said unto him, Gird thyself, and bind on thy sandals: and he did so. And he saith unto him, Cast thy garments about thee and follow me. And he went out and followed him, and wist not that it was true which was done by the angel, but thought he saw a vision."

The angelic deliverer guides him through the first and second ward to the iron gate of the city; it opens of its own accord; the apostle finds himself alone in the street, and blessing God for liberty, makes his way to the house in which the disciples are engaged in fervent supplication for him, and suddenly brings the answer to their prayer, by appearing in the midst of them. To the Gentile Cornelius, inquiring the way of life, the angel of the Lord appeared, bidding him send for Simon Peter, and when in obedience to the command of God the apostle came, the Holy Ghost fell on all them that heard the word, and thus the first converts were gathered from the Gentiles, and they were baptized in the name of the Lord. Throughout the New Testament, the doctrine of angelic agency is repeatedly maintained, either by examples asserting its actual exercise, or by distinct affirmation of its reality. Look at the little children whom Jesus blessed. How many perils beset the helpless infant; what fierce diseases wait around, and how much of the preservation of these little ones is due instrumentally to holy angels, we know not, but we do know that our Saviour says, "Their angels do always behold the face of my Father which is in heaven." Waiting, watching continually, ever on the wing to fly on some errand of mercy, they guard our tender years, and from the cradle to the grave, minister to the heirs of salvation, to keep them in all the dangers of the way. They crowd around us in the walks of life; in the daily avocations of business, amid the temptations of the world and of the great enemy, they are at our side. When the soldier of Christ encounters a host, as strong and cruel as the Syrian army, let him not think he is alone, for the mountains round about him are covered with horses and chariots of fire; the glorious legions of heaven are in array to help and guard him whilst he fights the good fight of faith. To the wicked they are often messengers of wrath. Thus the angel of God smote Herod when the people shouted in answer to his speech and profanely cried, "It is the voice of God and not of man," and he was eaten of worms and gave up the ghost. God's judgment upon persecutors and upon enemies of the truth has often been executed by holy angels. They sympathize in all God's administration, and the highest honour which they crave is to fulfil his purposes, their greatest delight is to do his holy will. Hence our Lord has taught us to pray, "Thy will be done on earth, as it is done in heaven."

CHAPTER IX.

THE ANGEL WATCHERS.

"During the which there was an heavenly noise
Heard sound through all the palace pleasantly,
Like as it had been many an angel's voice
Singing before th' Eternal majesty,
In their trinal triplicities on high;
Yet wist no creature whence that heavenly sweet
Proceeded, yet each one felt secretly
Himself thereby reft of his senses meet,
And ravished with rare impression in his sprite."

WHEN we go up to the house of God, angels go with us. How dreadful is the place where Christians meet to pray and praise. It is none other than the gate of heaven! When the sons of God come together to present themselves before the Lord, Satan comes also. When the sowers go forth bearing the precious seed of the kingdom, like the fowls of the air, the spirits of darkness are ready to catch up the seed that falls by the way-side. They distract the mind, call away the attention and seek to keep the truth from lodging in the heart. "Then cometh the devil and taketh away the word out of their hearts, lest they should believe and be saved;" (Luke viii. 12,) but at every point the legions of darkness are met by the blessed messengers of light, and when the penitential tear trembles upon the eyelids of the thoughtful prodigal, when afar off the publican stands, with downcast eyes, and smites upon his breast and cries, "God be merciful to me a sinner!" when the startled sinner exclaims in the anguish of his soul, "What must I do to be saved?" and the heart is filled with faith in Jesus, and the hand is fixed upon the cross of Christ, oh! there is joy in heaven, and thousand thousands voices, unheard by human ears, sing the song of Moses and the Lamb, and praise God that righteousness and peace have kissed each other, and that another soul redeemed has turned from the highway of death to seek the Saviour's face in glory. But, there is an hour, the great crisis of the believer's history on earth, when all the sympathies of earth and heaven cluster round him. When the poor body faints in death, and the soul, long weary and vexed with the vanities of a wicked world, pauses ere it leaves the clay breathless, and the last pangs that shall ever distress the departing pilgrim, are rending the feeble ties that bind the incorruptible to the spoils of death; oh! how human piety yearns over the sufferer, and all that affection's kindest ministrations can do, to assuage the parting agony is done, amid tears and anguish that all avails so little; but these are not the only watchers of the mortal strife. Angels are in that room—it is radiant with a glory which we cannot see, and which these dim eyes could not endure. They have kept the believing pilgrim in all his ways, and they come at last to guard his entrance into life, and through the dark, iron gate of death to lead him forth from the prison and clasp him in their sweet embrace, as they mount on wings of love and bear him upward to his Father's house. Marvel not, that when your bosom heaves with tumultuous grief, the last expression on the countenance of the dying Christian is the symbol of unutterable peace. He has a vision of angels; he hears them sweetly whisper. "Come away—thy work is done—the conflict is past, come enter into rest;" and the beaming smile of joy tells when all is over, and the fluttering heart is still, "All is well—all is well!"

Beloved reader, is it well with you? Many a friend has sickened and fallen at your side, and you have seen the dark grave open and enclose lover and acquaintance in its cold embrace, and still you live. Are you ready to depart? This is not your rest. You have seen, since you have been a pilgrim, you have seen the old man faint, and young men sink in mortal weariness; and thousands, many thousands, have been borne from their homes and carried through these streets, and in all these scenes of death and mourning, can you not read the tokens of your own approaching decease? Will you give all your care and thought to a wretched world which can only give you in exchange, a narrow grave? Oh! look up! look up! see the bright heaven above you. Think of Mount Zion. Think of the innumerable company of angels and the spirits of just men made perfect. Think of Christ, the mediator of the New Covenant! Believe in him, that it may be well with you.

2 CORINTHIANS V. 8.

We are confident, I say, and willing rather to be absent from the body, and to be present with the Lord.

ABSENT FROM THE BODY, PRESENT WITH THE LORD.

THIS is the language of strong faith. The things which are not seen and which are eternal must have affected the mind of the apostle with great power, in order to enable him to speak thus confidently. Paul lived for immortality. He kept eternity continually in view. His writings abound in similar expressions of readiness to depart and of desire to be with Christ. His conversation was in heaven. His treasure was in heaven, and his heart was there also. To the weeping elders at Miletus, sorrowing because they should see his face no more, he spoke with the same unwavering confidence, though the tenderest emotions were struggling for utterance: "And now, behold, I go bound in the spirit to Jerusalem, not knowing the things that shall befall me there; save that the Holy Ghost witnesseth in every city, saying that bonds and afflictions abide me. But none of these things move me; neither count I my life dear unto myself, so that I might finish my course with joy, and the ministry which I have received of the Lord Jesus, to testify the gospel of the grace of God." (Acts xx. 22–24.)

When he wrote to the Church at Phillipi from his prison at Rome, he tells his children in the gospel, that it is his earnest expectation and hope, that in nothing he shall be ashamed, but that with all boldness, as always, so now also, Christ shall be magnified in his body, whether it be by life or by death, and then adds those memorable words: "For, to me to live is Christ, and to die is gain. But if I live in the flesh, this is the fruit of my labour;" *i. e.*, I know that if I continue here, I shall gain more souls for Christ, "but what I shall choose, I know not, for I am in a strait betwixt two, having a desire to depart and to be with Christ which is far better. Nevertheless, to abide in the flesh is more needful for you." (Phil. i. 20–24.)

This language beautifully exemplifies the character of a child of God. Heavenly-minded, his affection is set on things above. He longs to be with Christ, and yet with quiet resignation to his Father's will he waits until his change comes. His constant prayer is, that Christ may be honoured in him, whether it be by life or by death. How few are prepared to look upon the tender ties that bind them to the world, to contemplate the rending of those bands which unite them to their family and kindred, and then calmly declare with the apostle, "We are willing rather to be absent from the body." How few can think of the inroads of disease, and anticipate the wasting of their frame upon a bed of pain and sickness and watch the silent advances of death, then urge the busy mind beyond the hour when the final struggle shall be over, see this body, cold and dead, and shrouded for the grave, and yet with confidence declare, "This is far better." But the apostle preferred to be absent from the body. He was as sensitive to pain, and naturally as averse to suffering as ourselves. He knew that ere he could depart to be with Christ, he must meet and conquer death, yet such was his trust in the power of his Redeemer, that he never faltered when the prospect was immediate. True, he tells the Corinthians in this chapter, that he did not desire to die for the sake of encountering death. If he groaned, being burdened in his earthly tent, it was not because he "would be unclothed, but clothed upon, that mortality might be swallowed up of life." (v. 4.) The grace of God had wrought within him that meetness for the heavenly inheritance which distinguishes the true believer. This it was that caused him to prefer heaven to earth, that made him choose rather to be absent from the body, that he might be present with the Lord. Let us endeavour to form a proper estimate of the force of the test, by showing the import of its terms.

1. *What is it to be absent from the body?* In our present state, our ideas are furnished through the medium of sense. We cannot readily conceive or appreciate a purely spiritual condition. The organs of the body are the instruments by which the soul so generally acts, that it is impossible for us to form an adequate idea of its separate existence. But this body, in its present form, is but a tent—a mere temporary covering of the soul. Perfect as its mechanism is, fearfully and wonderfully made, with all its nice adaptation to the functions of life, it must soon be broken up and laid down to moulder in the grave, "Earth to earth, dust to dust, ashes to ashes." The spirit dislodged will then return to God who gave it. Like the broken strings of a harp, which refuse to answer the touch of the skilful musician, the organs of sense will cease to vibrate under the emotions of the soul. The eye will see no more—the ear will be deaf—the tongue will be mute—the sealed lips will cease to be the door of utterance—the hand will forget its cunning—the limbs will be motionless, and much as this body has been loved and ever-loved, it must be carried away and buried out of sight. When absent from the body, *the soul will cease to derive gratification from the external sensual pleasures of this life.* The sense of enjoyment now conveyed to the mind

through the external organs will cease. Absent from the body, we taste no sweetness in food—no refreshment in repose. The possession of houses, and lands, of gold and silver, can afford no gratification to the soul. The affections of the heart could never be set upon them, except through the medium of the body. The soul in its separate state can derive no comfort from them. Therefore, the rich man who said to his soul, "Thou hast much goods laid up for many years, take thine ease, eat, drink, and be merry," was justly branded as "a fool." For when God says, "This night shall thy soul be required of thee, then whose shall these things be?" We brought nothing with us into this world, and it is certain we can carry nothing out. All the enjoyments of sense are but for a season. Regulated by grace, they are not all sinful, but they become a snare, they become pleasures of sin when the heart is set inordinately upon them. Though the soul retains its character, when it leaves the body and has all the appetites and propensities which constituted its ruling passion, whilst the union lasted, after its dissolution, it can derive no more gratification from temporal enjoyments, than if these things had never existed.

When absent from the body, the soul will derive no delight from many sources of intellectual and spiritual pleasure which are open to us now. The man of studious mind must leave his books. The pages which he once perused with so much enjoyment and profit are henceforth blank to him. He trims the midnight lamp no longer. He searches the sacred oracles of God no more. The pleasure which he enjoyed in the conversation of the wise and good with whom he associated, whom he cherished as his friends, and who survive him, is suspended. With them who go together to the house of God, he takes sweet counsel no longer. Though endeared by the most tender associations to those who worship there, he prays with them and for them, and unites in the songs of Zion no more. His soul may be knit to theirs as the soul of Jonathan was to David, but death severs *all* earthly ties for a season, and severs many for ever. It is sweet to listen to the teachings of God's word and to sit under the droppings of the sanctuary. To join in exalting the right hand of the Lord in the tabernacles of the righteous, is a blessed privilege. Dear to the child of God is the day of sacred rest—precious the assembly of God's saints. He loves the solemn anthems of praise. His heart and flesh cry out for the living God, and with the fervour of the Psalmist he can declare, "A day in thy courts is better than a thousand. I had rather be a door-keeper in the house of my God than to dwell in the tents of wickedness." But, *absent from the body*, he meets his brethren and companions in the earthly Zion no more. The place which once knew him in the sanctuary, and in the place of prayer, knows him no more for ever. His body reposes with the congregation of the dead, and his spirit returns to God.

When absent from the body, the soul can find no gratification in the discharge of those relative duties which are temporal. Whilst in the flesh, opportunities are afforded of doing good to others in a thousand various ways. We may relieve the wants of the needy, and alleviate sorrow and distress by kindness and sympathy, but these opportunities are all buried in the grave. If we would visit the fatherless children and the widows in their affliction, and make the heart of the desolate sing for joy, we must perform these works of mercy before the earthly house of this tabernacle is dissolved. The blessing of him that is ready to perish, comes not upon the dead, save in grateful remembrance of deeds of mercy which they can no longer perform. There are no poor in heaven, who may be warmed and fed by Christian beneficence; they are safe from hunger, thirst and pain—the sun shall not smite them by day, neither any heat, nor shall they ever be chilled by the frosts of winter, pinched by poverty or wearied by sickness. Christ feeds them with the hidden manna; the Lamb that is in the midst of the throne leads them to fountains of living water, and God wipes away all tears from their eyes. But here, the unequal allotments of Divine Providence are designed to afford opportunities for the exercise of Christian love. Here we may weep with them that weep. There we shall rejoice with them that do rejoice.

When absent from the body, we shall have no more opportunities of winning souls for Christ. This is the greatest honour which God puts upon his people here, and "Herein is my Father glorified," says Christ, "that ye bear much fruit." The believer, whilst present in the body, may be the instrument of salvation to multitudes. His personal entreaties and godly example, with God's blessing, may persuade a father or a mother to be reconciled to God, and his prayers may prevail with Christ in behalf of erring brethren and sisters, for Christ gives the Holy Spirit to them that ask him. He sends convincing and converting power to seal the testimony of faith, and listens to the fervent inwrought prayer of the righteous man. He sends his blessing upon the humble supplicant, who, like her of old, comes trembling yet believing, and falls at his feet with the earnest cry, "Lord, help me!"

The promises which assure the child of God, that Christ is ready to dispense his blessing, are to be pleaded now. They who are absent from the body have exchanged the voice of supplication for the song of praise to Him who loved them, and washed them from their sins in his own blood. All that we do in winning souls for Christ, must be done whilst we are absent from the Lord. The promise, "They that are wise shall shine as the brightness of the firmament, and they that turn many to righteousness as the stars for ever and ever," is given to encourage them who sow in tears, and gladden their hearts with the certain prospect, that they shall come again with rejoicing, bringing their sheaves with them. Surely this is a precious privilege! It was this that reconciled the apostles to the toil and privations of their office. "If I live in the flesh, this," says St. Paul, "is the fruit of my labour." He deemed life precious, because whilst the day lasted, he could preach Jesus and the resurrection, and from house to house warn men with tears, and as Christ's ambassador, beseech them to be reconciled to God. "Brethren, if any of you do err from the truth, and one convert him, let him know that he which converteth the sinner from the error of his way shall save a soul from death, and shall hide a multitude of sins." James v. 19, 20.) What man ever realized more deeply the import of this solemn truth than the apostle Paul? Who has ever been better prepared to appreciate the privilege of being a worker together with God, than this devoted servant of Christ? Yet he says, "We are willing rather to be absent from the body and present with the Lord. Literally, "We are well pleased" to be thus absent from the body; and again he says, "I desire to depart and to be with Christ, which is far better." The justness of this preference will appear if we consider,

II. *What it is to be present with the Lord.* Jesus Christ has given the promise to his people, "Lo, I am with you alway, even unto the end of the world;" but this is not spoken of his human, but of his divine presence. By his eternal power and Godhead he sustains and succours his believing people to the end of time. In the language of the Heidelberg Catechism, we say: "Christ is very man and very God; with respect to his human nature, he is no more on earth; but with respect to his Godhead, majesty, grace and spirit, he is at no time absent from us." This does not involve a separation of the two natures in Christ. This objection is obviated in our symbolical book, in these words: "If his human nature is not present, whenever his Godhead is, are not then these two natures in Christ separated from one another?" Answer. "Not at all; for since the Godhead is incomprehensible and omnipresent, it must necessarily follow, that the same is not limited with the human nature he assumed, and yet remains personally united to it." Therefore, when we speak of Christ's presence with his people on earth, we affirm it of his eternal power and Godhead. His bodily absence from his militant Church, is supplied by the presence of the Holy Ghost, in his comforting and quickening influence But "to be present with the Lord," implies that we shall behold him in his humanity, and dwell with him in glory. When this earthly house is dissolved, the soul of the believer enters into rest. "Blessed are the dead that die in the Lord from henceforth; yea, saith the Spirit, for they rest from their labours and their works do follow them." There is no delay, he is blessed from henceforth, immediately. So soon as his eyes close upon the scenes which gather round his dying bed, they open upon the bright glories of the upper world. Oh! what a glorious exchange is this! Who would not leave the crumbling tenement in which we dwell, whilst we are at home in the body, for a mansion in our Father's house? Christ has prepared a place for all who love him, and a crown for all who are faithful unto death. What a contrast between the weeping group who surround the couch on which the ruins of the earthly house repose and the rejoicing myriads of redeemed and happy spirits, who crowd around the departed saint, meeting the angels who convey him to Abraham's bosom, with shouts of joyous welcome! Whilst the voice of wailing and lamentation is loud in the dwelling which the angel of death has visited, and hearts are stricken and pierced with the bitterness of grief, a new song of praise is ascending to the Lamb slain, and another voice has learned the anthem of the thousands who stand on Mount Sion and follow the Lamb whithersoever he goeth. They who walk by sight, look upon the emaciated face—the hollow, sunken eyes—the lips mute and still as marble—and the soul recoils with horror; but faith gazes not upon the work of death; faith sees the liberated spirit dwelling within the pearly gates of the New Jerusalem, happy in the enjoyment of eternal pleasures, and faith pauses not, but says, "We are well pleased to be absent from the body and present with the Lord!" Faith looks from the tomb of nature to the sepulchre in Joseph's garden, and though the eyes may be dimmed with tears, and the voice falter with emotion, faith publishes the words of Christ, "I am the resurrection and the life! He that believeth on me, though he were dead, yet shall he live; and he that liveth and believeth in me shall never die." "Marvel not at this, for the hour is coming, in which all who are in the graves shall hear his voice and shall come forth, they that have done good to the resurrection of life." And it may well reconcile us to the allotments of divine providence in the departure of God's children, when we reflect, that *they are fulfilling the will of God.* So he who loves his children has decreed. We are not our own. We have solemnly covenanted to be the Lord's, and thus our times and all the changes of our earthly lot have been committed to his direction. It is the Christian's comfort in life and death that he belongs to his faithful Lord and Saviour, Jesus Christ. Whether we live, or whether we die, we are the Lord's, and when he appoints the hour of our last great change, we know that his will is always best. He who has guided the Christian pilgrim in all his journeyings through the wilderness is with him in the swellings of Jordan. The same voice which spoke words of comfort in seasons of darkness and cheered him in times of peril, bids him "go forward," and whispers, "fear not, for I am with thee." But apart from these general grounds of encouragement, there are special advantages which more than counterbalance all the temporal privileges which the believer enjoys whilst present in the body. It is true, he ceases to derive gratification from the enjoyments of sense; but there are rivers of joy at God's right hand and pleasures for evermore, of which he could form no conception whilst absent from the Lord. These flow from the throne of God and the Lamb in a living stream, and his soul is ravished with joys unutterable. The fountain from which they gush can never be exhausted: the pleasures they afford will never pall upon the taste. There are no dregs of bitterness in the cup of salvation. Absent from the body, the believer enters abundantly into life. He exchanges his portion upon earth for an exceeding and eternal weight of glory. Happy exchange! He is forever with the Lord.

It is admitted, that the death of the body seals up many sources of intellectual and spiritual improvement, but then it opens new treasures of heavenly knowledge which are inaccessible to them who are at home in the body. It confers advantages incomparably superior. Who can estimate the glorious increase of knowledge which they obtain, who are present with the Lord? The apostle Paul compares the intellectual strength of the believer at home in the body contrasted with the attainments of the heavenly state, with the respective acquirements of childhood and maturity. "For we know in part and we prophesy in part. But when that which is perfect is come, then that which is in part shall be done away. When I was a child, I spake as a child, I understood as a child, I thought as a child, but when I became a man I put away childish things. For now we see through a glass darkly, but then, face to face; now I know in part, but then shall I know, even I also am known."—(1 Cor. xiii. 9–12.) The soul will be freed from the clogs by which its progress in divine knowledge is now so much impeded. "Much study is a weariness of the flesh." The mental energies are unwearied, but the bodily organs through which they act are soon exhausted and require repose. When the faculties of the redeemed soul, radiant with the light and glory of heaven, shall enter upon the contemplation of the divine perfections, to what heights of excellent knowledge will they soar! How will the mysteries of grace and the dispensations of providence unfold new views of the divine wisdom and awaken the song of thankful acknowledgment, "Just and true are thy ways, thou King of Saints." Then it will be seen, that it was the hand of mercy which gathered clouds and darkness around the throne, and wrapped the dispensations of providence in mystery. He veils his purposes from us, because whilst we are present in the body, the full realization of them would be more than we could bear. Here, too, we are to walk by faith; but how could we exercise this virtue if there were no difficulties to encounter and surmount? There, we walk by sight. There we know, even as we are known. The pilgrim who has reached his home lays down the staff of faith at the threshold of his Father's house. Henceforth, he sees Jesus as he is, and is like his Saviour. Now he goes from grace to grace, but then from glory to glory, changed by the Spirit of the Lord. Finally, we say:

The employment of the heavenly state will be suited to the nature of the disembodied spirit. We shall not be idle in heaven. Our faculties will all be engaged in the service of God and the Lamb, and though there are none in the New Jerusalem whom we may instruct in the way of salvation, or lead as penitent sinners to the cross of Christ, there may be other worlds to which, on errands of love, the spirits of the just may speed in company with the angels of God. When we are removed from the fellowship of the saints on earth and can no more give thanks to God in these earthly courts, there is a bright, glorious, and innumerable company of angels, in whose ranks we may mingle, with whom we may exchange the greetings of heavenly friendship, and hear them tell of their ministry to the heirs of salvation. And then the spirits of the just made perfect are there. Moses and Samuel, with all the prophets of the Lord; Abraham and all the patriarchs who saw the promises afar off, and walked and lived and died in faith; Abel, the first martyr, and all who were slain for the word of God and the testimony of Jesus; Paul and his fellow apostles in the kingdom and patience of Christ; all—all are there! All who love the Saviour, whom we leave when we depart to be with Christ, shall follow at the Master's call, and until the Lord shall come in heavenly glory, all who shall hereafter believe on the name of Christ, shall be brought in their season to the habitations of eternal peace. Thus our fellowship is only suspended; it shall be renewed, for the communion of the saints is everlasting. There shall be one fold and one Shepherd. To the Christian, the great attraction of heaven is Christ. Many who speak of heaven and express their desire for its society, think of it only as associated with some departed one whom they have fondly loved, but to the child of God, the brightest hope of glory is that which flows from the knowledge that he shall see *Jesus.* If he desires to depart, it is that he may be with Christ. He would be absent from the body that he may be present with the Lord.

It is the privilege of the believer, who by faith is one with Christ, thus to desire to be clothed upon with his house, which is from heaven. Unless you are Christ's it will not profit you to be absent from the body. If you are the enemy of God, no greater calamity could befal you, than to be summoned into his presence.

Great God! on what a slender thread,
Hang everlasting things;
The eternal state of all the dead,
Upon life's feeble strings!

Oh! seek the Lord while he may be found. Lay hold upon the hope of the gospel, that when the Son of Man shall come, you may be found watching at the gate with them that love his appearing.

VALUABLE WORKS

RECENTLY ISSUED.

A Voice from the Pious Dead of the Medical Profeſſion;

Or, Memoirs of Eminent Physicians who have fallen asleep in Jesus; with a Preliminary Dissertation on the Cross as the Key to all Knowledge. By Henry J. Brown, A. M., M. D. Price, 90 cts.

NOTICES.

From Thomas E. Bond, M. D., Editor Christian Advocate & Journal, New York.—* * * * * We hail with joy the work before us. The author has done good service by showing examples of Christian belief and practice among the most eminent of the faculty, both in Europe and America. We especially recommend this work to our brethren of the Medical Profession. They will find, especially in the dissertations which precede the Memoirs, a fair exhibition of the peculiar difficulties which the study and practice of medicine and surgery present to the theory of Christianity; and are able and satisfactory solutions of these difficulties.

From G. C. M. Roberts, M.D., Baltimore.—After having carefully read the book, and *re-read portions of it*, with increased interest, I take great pleasure in returning you my sincere thanks for affording me the opportunity, through you, of commending it most earnestly to the community at large, and to the members of the Medical Profession in particular. At this particular juncture, when strenuous efforts are in progress for the purpose of elevating the standard of medical education throughout the land, this excellent Memoir of some among the most distinguished physicians, who have died in Christ, appears most opportunely. I trust you will be successful in placing a copy of it in the library of every medical man in our country; where it will not only prove the means of spiritual benefit to preceptors, but likewise to those who may be under their supervision.

From the Boston Medical & Surgical Journal.—This volume is written with a view "to refute a charge of incompatibility between the Christian religion and science, sometimes made by wicked and ignorant persons." It contains three short Dissertations on the subjects of The Cross in the Life-Union, The Cross in Nature, and The Cross in Medicine; which are followed by Memoirs of Wm. Hey, Dr. Hope, Dr. Good, Dr. Bateman, Dr. Godman, Dr. Gordon, Dr. Broughton, and Dr. Capadose. The Dissertations are intended "as an incentive to inquiry suggestive of a form." The Memoirs are interesting; and fully prove, what hardly requires proof, that there is nothing in science which tends to lessen men's faith in the Divine doctrines of the Christian Revelation, or deter them from fulfilling all its obligations. Dr. Brown's book will doubtless be read with interest by many who are not members of the profession, as well as by physicians.

From the Christian Observer, Philadelphia.—It affords us pleasure to call attention to this interesting volume. It contains an impressive argument for the truth and excellence of the Gospel, drawn from the lives of scientific men. It shows that faith in the teaching of the Scriptures is not merely a persuasion, but a power, stronger than the innate passions of our nature—a Divine power manifested in the development of all that is pure and lovely and of good report in real life. The memorials of these excellent men show conclusively, that science and religion are not, as a few sciolists have imagined, incompatible with each other. The Preliminary Dissertation is rich in thought, suggestive, adapted to awaken inquiry on the most important subject.

From the Western Christian Advocate, Cincinnati.—No book of a similar character is before the American public, and we trust it will find a good sale, not among physicians merely, but among all lovers of healthy, religious biography.

From the Pittsburg Christian Advocate.—The narrative of the closing scenes in the life of Dr. Gordon, of Hull, is of itself worth double the price of the book. Medical men, whose time is necessarily engrossed with professional engagements, will appreciate the aim of the author in collecting and condensing more extended memoirs of their worthy brothers in similar toils; and when they would not take up a long and laboured production, they can find in this volume that which will refresh and strengthen in the midst of their unceasing labours. Ministers and others, who sometimes wish to testify their high appreciation of the faithful services of the physician, will recognise in this volume a testimonial which cannot but be regarded as beautiful, appropriate, and valuable.

From the Christian Chronicle, Philadelphia.—The object of these pages is to show that there is a harmony between religion and science. It is decidedly a religious book, abounding with the most useful lessons from the highest authority. The Dissertation that precedes is a valuable production, much enhancing the value of the work.

From the National Magazine, New York and Cincinnati.—We commend the volume to the general reader; while, in the language of the preface, "To medical men of every class, these Memoirs come with singular force, involving, as they do, the modes of thought, the associations, and the difficulties common to the medical profession. Their testimony is as the united voice of brethren of the same toils, proclaiming a heavenly rest to the weary pilgrim. It comes, too, unembarrassed with any considerations of interest, or mere purpose of sect or calling."

From Rev. J. F. Berg, D. D.—The selection of a number of Memoirs of Physicians eminent for their piety, who have adorned their profession in our own country and in other lands, as examples of the living power of piety, is itself a happy thought; and the primary Dissertation on the Cross as the Key to all Knowledge will suggest valuable reflections to the mind of the thoughtful reader. It is an able presentation of the great theme of the Cross of Christ as the foundation of all genuine science.

The Bible Defended againſt the Objections of Infidelity.

Being an Examination of the Scientific, Historical, Chronological, and other Scripture Difficulties. By Rev. Wm. H. Brisbane. Price, 50 cts.

NOTICES.

From the Western Christian Advocate.—The work is on a plan somewhat original, and meets a want long felt by Sabbath School Teachers and Scholars, private Christians and others. We can most heartily commend the little manual to all seeking the truth as it is in the Gospel of Christ.

From the Christian Advocate & Journal.—The author, in the body of his work, commencing with the account of the Creation, as given in the book of Genesis, goes through the principal facts recorded in the Old and New Testaments, stating and answering the objections of infidelity cogently and logically, bringing to his aid the result of extensive reading and patient investigation. It is a small book,—so small that none will be deterred from reading it by its size: yet it condenses the most general objections to the Bible, with a clear statement of the refutation of them, by the best authors who have written on the subject.

From the National Magazine.—A small but good review of the chief infidel objections to the Bible has been published by Higgins & Perkinpine. It is by Rev. W. H. Brisbane, and examines the scientific, historical, chronological, and other difficulties alleged against the Scriptures. It is especially adapted to meet the wants of Sunday School and Bible Class Teachers.

From the Easton Star.—The title page indicates the character of this little volume, which has evidently been prepared with great care, by one who appears to have thoroughly investigated the subject, and whose researches well qualify him to elucidate the difficult questions reviewed. The style is chaste, perspicuous, and comprehensive, and the volume replete with original thoughts and pertinent quotations from the first biblical and scientific authors, to support the Divine authority of the Scriptures and refute the objections of sceptics. The book contains in a nutshell most of the points of difference be

Standard and Rare Books

IN EVERY

DEPARTMENT OF USEFUL KNOWLEDGE.

THEOLOGICAL.—A large and general aſſortment, embracing standard works in Theology, Eccleſiaſtical Hiſtory, Biblical Literature, Practical Religion, &c.; together with a fine collection of

PULPIT, FAMILY, AND POCKET BIBLES,

In varied and elegant ſtyles of binding and at every price.

SCIENTIFIC.—Compriſing works on Natural Science, Medicine, Mental and Moral Philoſophy, Political Economy, &c.

HISTORICAL & MISCELLANEOUS.—Ancient and Modern Hiſtory, Geography, Claſſical Antiquities and Literature, Travels, Biographies, &c.

SUNDAY SCHOOL BOOKS.—A very extenſive ſtock of Juvenile Works, ſelected with great care, and with ſpecial regard to the wants of Sabbath Schools, compriſing the collections of the Methodiſt Book Concern, New York, and that of the American Sunday School Union and American Tract Society. The terms the ſame as at their depoſitories.

All orders promptly attended to.

6

www.ingramcontent.com/pod-product-compliance
Lightning Source LLC
LaVergne TN
LVHW010234110826
845151LV00004B/1286
* 9 7 8 1 4 2 5 5 2 5 2 2 4 *